Agricultural Policy and Collective Self-Reliance in the Caribbean

Barb: expansive measures = laissez faire
distrib   "   = dirigiste (p. 29)

About the Book and Author

Focusing on the process of agricultural policy-making within the Caribbean Community and Common Market (CARICOM), this book provides a context for understanding the evolving theory of regional integration among developing countries. Dr. Axline traces the progress of Caribbean integration from its beginnings in the mid-1960s to its present state of stagnation. Drawing on original documents and extensive interviews in the twelve CARICOM member countries, he describes the move away from a market-oriented *laissez-faire* approach to agriculture and the shift toward sectoral programming. The role of other regional organizations, such as the Caribbean Development Bank and the Caribbean Agricultural Research and Development Institute, is examined and related to national and regional policies in the agricultural sector. The Caribbean experience, concludes Dr. Axline, suggests that the future direction of regional cooperation among developing countries will likely be toward more intensive integration on a less extensive scale.

W. Andrew Axline is professor of political science at the University of Ottawa. He has published works on regional integration in Europe, Latin America, Africa, and the Caribbean. Since 1974 he has carried out extensive field research in the Caribbean and at present is engaged in research on the South Pacific as part of a comparative study of regional cooperation.

This book has been published
with the help of a grant from
the Social Science Federation of Canada,
using funds provided by
the Social Sciences and Humanities Research Council of Canada

Agricultural Policy and Collective Self-Reliance in the Caribbean

W. Andrew Axline

Westview Press / Boulder and London

Westview Special Studies on Latin America and the Caribbean

Copyright © 1986 by Westview Press, Inc.

Published in 1986 in the United States of America by Westview Press, Inc.; Frederick A. Praeger, Publisher; 5500 Central Avenue., Boulder, CO 80301

Library of Congress Cataloging in Publication Data
Axline, W. Andrew.
  Agricultural policy and collective self-reliance in
the Caribbean.
  (Westview special studies on Latin America and the
Caribbean)
  1. Agriculture and state—Caribbean Area.
2. Caribbean Area—Economic integration. I. Title.
HD1831.Z895 1984   338.1′81′091821   84-15263
ISBN 0-86531-836-0

Printed and bound in the United States of America

The paper used in this publication meets the minimum requirements of the American National Standard for Permanence of Paper for Printed Library Materials
Z39.48-1984.

10   9   8   7   6   5   4   3   2   1

For Ailsa Gillian, my wife

Contents

Tables

Preface

The present study is the result of research carried out over a number of years and the culmination of the evolution of my thinking about the process of regional integration among developing countries. It is limited to a descriptive analysis of the adoption of regional agricultural policy among the states that constitute the Caribbean Community and Common Market. By choosing to study policy-making within a single economic sector in a particular region, I have sacrificed a certain amount of generality in favor of the detail that can be provided by such a case study. However, by carrying out the study within a clearly defined theoretical framework, I hope that lessons can be drawn regarding the development of agricultural policy on a regional basis and the progress of regional integration among developing countries in general.

Attempts by the member states of CARICOM over the past few years to use the regional organization to address the fundamental problems of declining agricultural production (both domestic and export), increasing food imports, and problems of nutrition provide the focus of the study. These regional activities are analyzed against the theoretical and historical background of colonialism, slavery, the plantation economy, and the move toward regional integration as a partial solution to the problems of underdevelopment and dependence.

No attempt has been made here to develop a theory of agricultural integration different from the general theoretical framework for understanding the broader process of regional integration among developing countries. Rather, activities in the agricultural sector are seen as part of the tendency for integration to proceed toward more intensive cooperation on a less extensive scale.

Unlike the traditional theory of customs unions, which focuses on the freeing of trade as a basis for regional integration, other types of policies are better adapted to less developed countries with relatively small industrial sectors. For these countries, a form of regional sectoral programming can offer benefits and provide the basis for negotiating regional agreements necessary for the adoption of policy on a region-wide basis. Regional agricultural policy in the Caribbean reflects this form of cooperation, particularly in its Regional Food and Nutrition Strategy and in the activities of the Caribbean Food Corporation.

To my knowledge, the Caribbean represents the most ambitious attempt on the part of developing countries to attack the fundamental problems of agriculture through regional cooperation. As such, it may prove to be a useful example for the study of other regions in addition to contributing to a theoretical understanding of regional integration.

The field research for this study was carried out during numerous visits to all twelve member countries of CARICOM over the past ten years; the documentary research was carried out at the Institute of Commonwealth Studies in London and the Institute of Development Studies at the University of Sussex in England. The major source of data on regional cooperation in the agricultural sector was provided by interviews with hundreds of officials of member governments, the CARICOM Secretariat, the Caribbean Development Bank and other regional institutions, farmers and members of farm organizations, agricultural marketing boards, and other individuals in the region. All of these people were unfailingly helpful and friendly in responding to my inquiries, and I owe them a great debt of gratitude, even though I must respect their anonymity. Of particular help were the librarians of the CARICOM Secretariat in Georgetown, the Caribbean Development Bank in Bridgetown, and the United Nations Economic Commission for Latin America, Office for the Caribbean, in Port of Spain. This research was funded by the Social Sciences and Humanities Research Council of Canada, without whose support the present project would have been impossible.

W. Andrew Axline

1
Introduction: The Setting for Caribbean Integration

The Commonwealth Caribbean extends from Guyana on the northeast coast of South America to Belize in Central America.[1] In between, stretching over thousands of miles, are the island territories, from Jamaica in the center of the Caribbean Sea to the republic of Trinidad and Tobago at its southeast extremity. North of Trinidad and Tobago, constituting part of the lesser Antilles of the East Caribbean, are the Leeward Islands of St. Kitts-Nevis, Antigua, and Montserrat, and the Windward Islands of Dominica, St. Lucia, St. Vincent, and Grenada. East of the Windward Islands is Barbados, jutting out into the South Atlantic ocean. The Bahamas, though a member state of the Caribbean Community, is not a participant in the Common Market, and thus does not figure in this analysis.

The Commonwealth Caribbean region as a whole is economically underdeveloped, given that all of the countries included in it are essentially primary producers, depending heavily on extractive industry and agriculture for export earnings. Tourism has begun to supplement these earnings in some countries, particularly Jamaica, Barbados, Antigua, and more recently St. Lucia. But in no country does manufacturing account for more than 15 percent of GDP. On the basis of the differences in levels of economic development within the region, Barbados, Guyana, Jamaica, and Trinidad and Tobago have been designated as the more developed countries (MDCs) and those remaining as the less developed countries (LDCs). Basic indicators for the Caribbean countries are provided in Table 1.1.

In the mid-1960s, just preceding the establishment of CARIFTA, the pattern of intra-Caribbean and international trade revealed the degree of dependency of the region, with dominant ties remaining to the United Kingdom (along former colonial lines) and, more recently, to the United States. In 1967, approximately 6 percent of total Caribbean exports went to other Caribbean countries, compared

Table 1.1

Basic Indicators for CARICOM Countries, 1980

	Less Developed Countries (LDCs)								More Developed Countries (MDCs)			
	Antigua	Dominica	Grenada	Montserrat	St. Kitts	St. Lucia	St. Vincent	Belize	Barbados	Guyana	Jamaica	Trinidad
Population (1980)	75,000	74,000	98,000	12,000	44,000	116,000	99,000	145,000	254,000	884,000	2,192,000	1,067,000
Area (m^2)	440	751	344	104	269	616	389	22,963	430	214,970	10,992	5,128
Density	170	99	285	115	164	188	254	6	591	4	199	208
GDP ($US million)	83	55	58	15	29	95	51	63	726	524	2,668	6,391
Per Capita GDP	1,102	742	590[a]	1,215	663[b]	820	512	436	2,859	592	1,217	5,990
Arable Land (hectares)	11,000	19,000	16,000	2,000	15,000	20,000	19,000	125,000	37,000	1,378,000	475,000	169,000
Density, Arable Land	7	4	6	6	3	6	5	1	7	1	5	6
Exchange Rate ($US)	0.37	0.37	0.37	0.37	0.37	0.37	0.37	0.50	0.50	0.39	0.56	0.42
Agriculture as percent of GDP	6.4	38.2	31.9[a]	6.6	18.5[b]	12.8	13.7	31.4	9.8	23.4	8.4	2.4
Manufacturing as percent of GDP	6.1	5.0	2.8[a]	7.4	14.8[b]	7.3	14.4	10.5	10.9	12.1	15.5	5.9
Mining as percent of GDP	0.8	0.7	0.1[a]	0.5	0.4[b]	1.6	0.3	0.3	0.8	16.5	14.3	41.9
Construction as percent of GDP	7.0	10.2	2.2[a]	13.5	6.2[b]	15.1	12.1	7.2	7.2	7.1	5.9	8.2
Transport, Distribution as percent of GDP	29.9	14.3	21.4[a]	25.9	19.7[b]	22.2	23.6	10.1	27.8	14.2	24.7	10.3
Government as percent of GDP	13.8	21.6	22.1[a]	21.6	20.8[b]	14.0	16.9	10.5	14.9	18.7	14.7	7.5
Other Sectors as percent of GDP	35.9	9.9	19.6[a]	24.6	19.5[b]	27.1	19.1	30.0	28.6	7.9	16.6	31.0

SOURCE: United Nations/Economic Commission for Latin America, Office for the Caribbean, Agricultural Statistics: Caribbean Countries, 1982 (Port of Spain, Trinidad and Tobago: ECLA, 1982), various tables.

[a] Data for 1979.
[b] Data for 1978.

to 20 percent to the United Kingdom and 35 percent to the United States.[2] Intra-Caribbean trade was limited to a very few commodities: petroleum and its products, rice, copra, coconut oil, fruits, and vegetables.

The institutions of the Caribbean Community and Common Market are intergovernmental, with none of the aspects of "supranational" decision making found in the European Community. The policy of the Community is determined by the Heads of Government Conference (HGC), which is the supreme decision-making organ. This conference meets several times a year, with each member country represented by the head of its government or designated alternate. Each member has one vote, and a unanimous vote is required to take decisions and make recommendations, the former of which are binding on the member states.

The principal organ of the Common Market is the Common Market Council of Ministers, which consists of one state minister or his or her alternate from each member country. With some minor exceptions, its decisions are also taken by unanimous vote. Normally a Council of Ministers meeting will immediately precede a meeting of the Heads of Government Conference, at which time the decisions of the former are ratified. The council will also convene between meetings of the HGC to deal with its principal responsibility—namely, the ongoing operations of the Common Market. The Council of Ministers meetings are often preceded by a meeting of the council with the Joint Consultative Group (JCG), which was established in 1971 to provide communication with the major economic groups in the region. The Caribbean Association of Industry and Commerce (CAIC), the Caribbean Congress of Labour (CCL), and the Caribbean Council of Consumers (CCC) have all participated in the Joint Consultative Group, but the Caribbean Association of Industry and Commerce has been the most active participant by far.

The Caribbean Community Secretariat, formerly the Commonwealth Caribbean Regional Secretariat, is the principal administrative organ of CARICOM. It operates under the accepted rule of international secretariats, in that its personnel may neither seek nor accept instructions from any national government, and its actions must be in the interest of the Community. The functions of the Secretariat are to service the meetings of the institutions and committees of CARICOM, implement the decisions of these meetings, initiate and carry out studies relating to regional integration and cooperation, provide member states the services they may request in order to achieve the objectives of the Community, and perform other duties that may be assigned by the Heads of Government Conference or other institutions of the Community.[3]

There are other specialized institutions of the Community responsible for the specific sectors of Health, Education, Labour, Foreign Affairs, Finance, Agriculture, and Mines.[4] In addition, the Treaty provides for the establishment of Associate Institutions of the Community; those established thus far are the Caribbean Development Bank (CDB); the Caribbean Investment Corporation (CIC); the Organization of East Caribbean States (OECS), formerly the West Indies Associated States (WISA) Council of Ministers; the East Caribbean Common Market (ECCM) Council of Ministers; the Caribbean Examinations Council; the Council of Legal Education; the University of Guyana; the University of the West Indies (UWI); the Caribbean Food Corporation (CFC); the Caribbean Meteorological Council; and the Regional Shipping Council.

Caribbean integration is taking place within this institutional structure. However, the real politics of integration is reflected in the bargaining and negotiations among member governments and other actors, which began with proposals to establish a free trade area in the region in the mid-1960s.

Hence the Commonwealth Caribbean provides a unique setting for the study of contemporary theory and policy relating to development issues. The Caribbean Community and Common Market (CARICOM) is a prime example of a group of small postcolonial countries involved in efforts to overcome the constraints of underdevelopment and dependency. These efforts are being made through policies combining a number of different approaches to development and reflecting the evolution of theory and practice over the past three decades. One of the most interesting features of development policy in the Caribbean is that it brings together under the aegis of formal regional institutions the concern with "basic needs"[5] as a basis for development and the approach of "collective self-reliance"[6] as a means of pursuing development goals. The evolution of regional integration from a liberal prescription for freeing trade to a positive framework for coordinating development policy qualifies it as a central example of collective self-reliance. And the emphasis within integration on satisfying regional food requirements represents a shift toward concern for basic needs. The concrete manifestation of the union of these two approaches is found in the regional policies that CARICOM is developing in the agricultural sector.

Although a study of regional policy in a single sector limited to the Caribbean provides a rather narrow focus, conclusions drawn from this analysis can shed light on the broader issues of the role of agriculture in development, the place of the agricultural sector in the overall process of integration, and the changing nature of regional integration among developing countries.

To understand fully the broader implications of CARICOM's agricultural policy for Third World regional integration, we must place it in the context of the change in theoretical emphasis that has taken place in recent years. Development needs have become more important, and marginal increases in efficiency, which are central to traditional customs union theory, have become less important. The form of integration has moved away from simple measures of liberalizing trade and toward a greater degree of policy coordination aimed at directly affecting conditions within the region and relations with third countries. This integration is reflected to a certain degree in the evolution of the general thrust of Caribbean integration over the past decade and a half, but it emerges most strikingly when recent efforts in the specific area of regional agricultural policy are analyzed.

CARICOM is in the process of formulating a comprehensive and ambitious regional program that goes far beyond what other integration schemes among developing countries have attempted. As such, CARICOM's agricultural policy may serve as a model for other regions, although it is too early to tell if it will be a model to emulate or one to avoid. In any event, there are certain useful lessons to be learned from the Caribbean example.

Of particular interest to the student of regional integration is the relationship between the progress of integration within the agricultural sector and the stagnation of the broader integration movement in the Caribbean. The present study leads to the conclusion that more intensive integration is possible when undertaken on a less extensive scale—in this case, the agricultural sector. The history of Caribbean agriculture, with its legacy of British colonialism, sugar cultivation, and slavery, is reflected strongly in present-day conditions in the region. This history represents a particular kind of dependent underdevelopment—the plantation economy—that conditions the region's relationship with the outside world and defines its place in the world economy. A knowledge of this history is no less important to understanding regional agricultural policy than is an understanding of regional integration theory. Hence the present study analyzes CARICOM's agricultural policy within the context of contemporary integration theory, the recent history of Caribbean integration, and existing conditions in the agricultural sector of the region.

In Chapter 2 I elaborate a general theoretical framework for integration among developing countries and examine the role of agriculture in integration. Chapter 3 contains an analysis of the progress of Caribbean integration from 1967 to the present, including an examination of the role of agricultural policy in the overall process of integration. Chapter 4 describes existing agricultural conditions in the region as they have evolved out of the history of colonialism and slavery. Chapter 5 presents a detailed analysis of the various policies that have been formulated by CARICOM in the agricultural sector, and in Chapter 6 some general conclusions are drawn concerning Caribbean integration in the agricultural sector.

Notes

1. The material from this section relies mainly on the official publications of the CARICOM Secretariat, principally *CARIFTA and the New Caribbean* (Georgetown, Guyana: CARIFTA, 1971); *From CARIFTA to Caribbean Community* (Georgetown, Guyana: CARIFTA, 1972); and *The Caribbean Community—A Guide* (Georgetown, Guyana: CARIFTA, 1973).

2. The relationship between dependence and lack of integration of the national economy is conceptualized in Havelock Brewster, "Economic Dependence: A Quantitative Interpretation," *Social and Economic Studies* 22 (March 1973):90–95.

3. *The Caribbean Community—A Guide,* pp. 68–69.

4. Ibid., pp. 66–68. For a detailed analysis of CARICOM institutions, see Hans Geiser, Pamela Alleyne, and Caroll Gajraj, *Legal Problems of Caribbean Integration: A Study on the Legal Problems of CARICOM* (Leiden, Holland: Sitjhoff, 1976). See also Kenneth Hall and Byron Blake, "The Caribbean Community: Administrative Aspects," *Journal of Common Market Studies* (March 1978):211–228.

5. The concern with basic needs as an important element of development was given a major impetus with the publication by the International Labor Office of *Employment, Growth, and Basic Needs: A One World Problem* (New York: Praeger Publishers, 1977), in which emphasis is placed on the fulfillment of the minimal food, clothing, housing, and health needs of the poorest segment of the population in underdeveloped countries.

6. "Collective self-reliance" refers to efforts at cooperation among developing countries on a South-South basis to achieve a redistribution of world production, control over the production and allocation of surplus in developing countries, and the power to make their own decisions on matters affecting their own societies. In effect, collective self-reliance strives to restructure or replace North-South links through the creation of new links among developing countries. See Enrique Oteiza, "Collective Self-Reliance: Some Old and New Issues," mimeo, Institute of Development Studies (IDS), University of Sussex, 1978. See also Enrique Oteiza, "Collective Self-Reliance Among Developing Countries," in Khadija Haq, ed., *Equality of Opportunity Within and Among Developing Countries* (New York: Praeger Publishers, 1977), pp. 81–87.

2
Regional Integration and the Agricultural Sector

There is an impressive volume of literature treating both the theory of integration among developing countries and the role of agriculture in economic development. However, there is little or no theoretical literature dealing specifically with agriculture in regional integration. The agricultural sector is generally treated as though it were subject to the same economic and political forces as other sectors of the economy and, therefore, as subject to the same analytical framework. In the analysis of regional integration among developing countries, agriculture has been largely ignored in favor of studies of industrialization; where it *has* been dealt with, it is treated as analogous to the industrial sector. This emphasis is understandable, but it has led to a neglect of one of the most important problems facing developing countries.

This study does not propose to develop a theoretical framework for the study of agriculture in integration; rather, it provides a detailed analysis of regional integration policy in the agricultural sector within a particular framework for the study of integration and development. CARICOM's agricultural policies are the most ambitious regional integration schemes among developing countries, which, for the most part, have relegated agriculture to a position of low priority in regional activities.

Agriculture in Integration

It seems paradoxical that the European Community—a region composed of highly industrialized economies in which agriculture accounts for a relatively small proportion of economic activity—has a very complex and comprehensive Common Agricultural Policy (CAP), whereas integration schemes among developing countries, which rely to a great degree on agricultural production, have few and very limited regional agricultural policies. Nearly all of the existing regional integration schemes do include agriculture, but for the most part policies in this area have lagged behind regional policies designed to promote industrial growth. Studies of comparative experiences of agriculture in integration virtually do not exist, and only very recently have tentative steps been taken by regional integration schemes to adopt and implement agricultural policies.[1] To say that agriculture has been a neglected aspect of regional integration among developing countries is not to say that it has been completely ignored, however. In fact, nearly all the existing regional and subregional integration schemes include agriculture within their scope.[2]

The provisions relating to agriculture in the defunct Latin American Free Trade Association (LAFTA) are found in Chapter 7, Articles 27–31 (Annex 1), of the Treaty of Montevideo. These very general provisions are mainly the expression of good intentions—designed, for example, to increase intraregional agricultural trade and to coordinate agricultural development policies for the better use of natural resources.[3] The treaty reflects the desire of the member countries to include agricultural production in the trade liberalization program while at the same time recognizing the difficulty of applying the classic principles of free competition to a sector marked by great differences among countries in the region in levels of productivity and in the organization and structure of the sector. As a compromise between these two principles, the treaty also recognizes the need for "special dispositions" regulating free trade in agricultural products.[4] Early in the integration experience, trade expansion was important for national import-substitution policies in LAFTA, but agricultural questions have contributed, overall, to delaying the process of trade liberalization in the region. There have been no modifications in the agricultural provisions of the Treaty of Montevideo since its beginning, although, at times, LAFTA studied the possibility of the harmonization and coordination of norms in the agricultural sector.[5]

In the Central American Common Market (CACM), as in other regional integration schemes, impressive increases in regional trade, including agriculture, have taken place. Yet, although most of the increase in imports pertained to products that can be produced in the region, not much trade diversion took place in agriculture primarily because of the emphasis placed on traditional agricultural exports.[6] One of the most significant shortcomings in the CACM has been the lack both of regional definition and of coordination of national production policies and programs in the agricultural sector. The only attempt to coordinate and implement national policies in the production, marketing, and regulation of intraregional agricultural trade has been limited to basic grains, and here the approach has moved from a regional to a bilateral one.[7]

In the early 1970s, a number of steps were taken to restructure the CACM, including the agricultural sector. At the end of 1974, a High-Level Committee agreed that the agricultural sector should receive priority in solving the problem of imbalance in the level of development of member countries; then, as a first step in this direction, the ministers of agriculture signed a "Plan of Action for the Production and Trade of Basic Grains in Central America" in 1975. It has been decided by the High-Level Committee that the new treaty establishing the Central American Economic and Social Committee must contain specific machinery for agricultural planning and programming, but also that the regional efforts of the CACM in the agricultural sector must remain essentially within the approach of trade liberalization.[8]

The basic provisions for agricultural integration in the Andean Group found in Chapter 7, Articles 69–74, of the Cartagena Agreement, were more ambitious than the goals set forth by LAFTA and CACM.[9] They contemplated the development of an agricultural policy through the adoption of an indicative plan for the agricultural sector, with the objectives of improving rural living conditions, increasing production and productivity through geographical and land-use specialization, and increasing foreign exchange earnings through import substitution and diversification of exports. These goals were to be pursued through the planning of agricultural development and joint programs of research. The ministers of agriculture in the Andean Group held their first meeting in January 1974 in Lima in an effort to reactivate and accelerate the progress of integration in the agricultural sector. They restated the need to coordinate national agricultural policy and to reach joint solutions to the problems of the underdevelopment of agriculture and the inadequacy of production.[10] In May 1974, the *Consejo Agropecuario* was created to oversee the harmonization and coordination of national policies and to prepare an action program in the agricultural sector.[11]

Although the Andean Group has gone farther than either LAFTA or CACM in encouraging agricultural complementarity among member countries,[12] progress in the integration of the sector has not been great, particularly in comparison to the aggressiveness that has been shown in the industrial sector. The idea of the Indicative Plan for Sectoral Development seems to have lost political force, and concrete accomplishments have been limited to solving specific problems of production, short supply, and third-country imports (i.e., imports from non-member states outside the region).[13]

Integration schemes among developing countries outside Latin America have seen even less progress toward regional policies in the agricultural sector, although a number of them have a specific mandate to adopt measures of one kind or another in the sector.[14] This relative neglect of integration in the agricultural sector is not surprising, however, when it is considered in the context of the main thrust of development policy in the 1950s and 1960s and, especially, in relation to the role of regional integration in development. Industrialization was conceived as the central process through which economic growth was to be stimulated, and national policies were directed mainly toward this end. Integration theory was almost exclusively concerned with the industrial sector and became attractive as a development strategy for precisely this reason. Any attempts to apply integration theory to agriculture were based on analogy rather than analysis, and were often included as an afterthought—usually through the application of trade-liberalization measures to agricultural products but without any attention given to the potential consequences.

The existing structure of the agricultural sector further reinforced this bias of integration policies toward industrialization. Typically, Latin American agriculture was dominated by the production of traditional export crops (bananas, sugar, cocoa, citrus, coffee, spices)—a sector that was vertically integrated through cultivation, planting, growing, harvesting, and shipping to a single metropolitan export market. The overwhelming proportion of fertile land, capital, technology, infrastructure, and skills relating to agriculture lay in this subsector. Little need or desire for regional integration was seen in traditional export agriculture.

Found alongside this subsector was local food production—part subsistence and part cash crop—which relied on a smaller amount of less fertile land, used little capital, and required low levels of technology, infrastructure, and skills. Contributing far less to GDP, and taking third place behind traditional export agriculture and the industrial sector, local food production received priority treatment neither in overall development policy nor within integration schemes. In addition, the strong influence of metropolitan powers on the direction of regional integration (particularly in Latin America and the Caribbean) and the important role played by the multinational corporations in the region favored policies that benefited these companies—policies concerned with the freeing of trade in industrial products combined with the benign neglect of agriculture. Finally, the general lack of political power among peasants relative to other political groups (large landowners, industrial and commercial forces) further reinforced the neglect of this sector.

Even though the major example of regional integration emulated by developing countries—the European Community—had embarked on an ambitious regional agricultural policy, the major thrust of this policy was to counter problems of surplus and overproduction, and thus the European experience was inapplicable as a model for developing countries. More recently, in the 1970s and 1980s, conditions have changed, thus bringing, in turn, a new interest among developing countries in regional integration within the agricultural sector. These changing conditions are found in the nature of the contemporary world economy and in more recent thinking about the role and nature of regional integration among developing countries.

Integration and Development:
The Evolution of Theory and Practice

CARICOM is only one of a number of integration schemes established in Latin America and other regions. Differences among these integration schemes, and changes within them, can be understood as reflections of the evolution of thinking about development and integration as a means to achieve it.[15]

Prescriptions for development based on neoclassical economic theory and programs of integration coming out of traditional customs union theory owe their great degree of compatibility to their shared origins in liberal *laissez-faire* economics. Based on a simplistic analogy with Great Britain during the Industrial Revolution, this approach saw unfettered free trade as the best means to bring about industrialization in the developing countries. International trade would serve as the "engine of growth," which along with foreign investment and aid would provide the much-needed capital to implant productive enterprises in these countries. The spin-off effects of forward and backward linkages and employment would eventually diffuse throughout the economy, thereby resulting in development. One of the major debates within this "diffusionist" approach to development occurred over the issue of balanced or unbalanced growth, which turned on the question of availability of capital and markets. International free trade and *laissez-faire* national policies are basic prescriptions of this approach.

Customs union theory presents regional economic integration as "second best" compared to global free trade, inasmuch as it represents a step away from individually protected national economies. Customs union theory is directly derived from neoclassical economics, and its principal benefits are based on increases in efficiency achieved by freeing trade—hence the emphasis on "gains from trade" and the central role occupied by the criterion of the net amount of trade creation over trade diversion as the main determinant of the beneficial results of a customs union.[16] The larger market and potential gains from trade resulting from economic integration, along with the stimulative example of the EEC, made it an obvious candidate as a policy to be adapted to a concept of development based on liberal economics. However, in the transfer of traditional customs union theory from Europe to developing areas, the importance of one crucial aspect of the theory was overlooked: The eventual goal of integration in an underdeveloped setting—namely, the creation of an industrialized economy—was a precondition of the theory. Customs union theory assumes the existence of an industrialized economy with full employment of factors of production in order for its beneficial effects to be realized. In addition, it specifies certain conditions (of size, significance of foreign trade, etc.) that are necessary if it is to generate the expected gains. Developing countries generally do not satisfy these conditions, thus leading some economic theorists to question the desirability of integration schemes among developing countries.[17] These theorists have realized that traditional customs union theory could not be transferred directly to regions like Latin America and Africa, but that it could be adapted to them. Such adaptation would involve a shift away from the conception of gains defined as increases in income through marginal growth in productivity to gains defined as the creation of new industrial activity using unemployed or under-utilized factors of production, even at relatively low levels of productivity. The real impetus for the adaptation of regional integration as a development strategy, however, came from the Economic Commission for Latin America (ECLA) doctrine of import-substituting industrialization developed by Raúl Prebisch.

In the 1950s and 1960s, development policies in Latin America and the Caribbean were greatly influenced by the ideas put forth by Raúl Prebisch and W. Arthur Lewis in their essays dealing with industrialization and development in the region.[18] Based on these ideas, the dominant theme in development strategy became import-substituting industrialization through the attraction of foreign investment. Popularly known as "industrialization by invitation," this strategy relies on a protected national market and fiscal incentives to attract industrial investment. Where these policies were seen to have exhausted their potential contribution to development at the national level, customs union theory provided a basis for their extension to the regional level. Trade diversion, an undesirable effect according to traditional customs union theory, became the goal of import substitution at the regional level, with the added inducements to investment of the larger regional market and common external tariff. The Economic

Commission for Latin America became a major proponent and promoter of this strategy and actively contributed to the establishment of LAFTA and CACM and, to a lesser degree, the Caribbean Free Trade Association (CARIFTA).

The doctrine of industrialization by invitation brought disappointments in addition to successes as increased foreign investment led to alienation of control of the economy, distortions in the labor market, large import bills for inputs, and expatriation of profits. At the regional level, these effects were often exacerbated by the greater ability of the multinational companies to take advantage of the larger protected market and the tendency of regional integration to reinforce and politicize existing inequalities among countries of the region. These developments confirmed the view of a number of critics who saw in the integration process an opening up of the economies to the exploitation of the multinational companies and even greater disintegration of the local economy.

The emphasis on regional integration as a market solution to economic development and its marriage to the doctrine of industrialization by invitation made it the object of harsh criticism on the part of scholars of the *dependencia* tradition.[19] When closely observed, the data that showed the "success" of regional integration in the form of an impressive expansion of trade revealed the large degree to which this trade was accounted for by multinationals and to which the "gains from trade" were concentrated in the more advanced member countries of the region.

The issues of unequal distribution of the gains from integration and polarization of industrial development within regional groupings were manifest in the earliest examples of Latin American and African integration, and some attempts were made to offset their impact. The issue of dependency arose later and led to a few attempts to define a regional policy to counter the problem, principally in the Andean Group and CARICOM. Both of these problems have been the source of the major political conflicts that have disrupted the process of regional integration throughout its history.

The problems of inequality and dependence, in addition to the highly politicized nature of these issues in developing countries, have required an approach to understanding integration that could not be satisfied by existing economic or political theories of integration. The historical and holistic nature of *dependencia* thinking, along with the shifting of the nature of integration toward a tool of policy coordination for economic development, gave rise to a political economy approach to regional integration.[20] Such a focus shifted attention away from the economic gains associated with free trade and political integration toward a sociopolitical analysis of developmental regionalism within the world economy.

Although nearly all regional integration schemes among developing countries are based on the establishment of a free trade area or a customs union, this trade-liberalization approach no longer reflects the major thrust of integration. In Latin America this situation is most evident in the Andean Group, which has gone furthest toward a system of sectoral programming—one example of integration policy well adapted to solving problems of development. This tendency is symptomatic of a trend in Third World regional integration toward more intensive integration on a less extensive scale, as characterized by the adoption of policies much more *dirigiste* in nature within a limited sector of activity, and perhaps among a smaller group of countries, in the form of subregional integration. The Andean Group's emergence as a subregional grouping out of LAFTA, and CARICOM's move toward a "deepening" rather than a "widening" of the integration movement are examples of this trend. Often the political compromises required to adopt these more advanced policies can be achieved only among a smaller grouping of states.

The reasons behind this trend become evident when one examines the various integration policies in the context of the requirements of regional integration for development. First, integration must bring about an increase in net benefits for the region. Second, it must provide for a distribution of those benefits that is satisfactory to all members of the region. And, third, it must contribute to the increased capacity of the region to maintain an internal dynamic of development, thus reducing the region's dependence on outside forces. Moreover, it must accomplish these tasks within the social, economic, and political conditions prevailing in developing countries.

Traditional customs union theory demonstrates how an economic union can achieve the first of these goals—that is, achievement of a real increase in welfare for the region as a whole. The requisite conditions of an industrialized economy and the lack of attention to intercountry distribution of gains have placed into question the role that this freeing-of-trade approach plays in integration among developing countries. If trade integration has a small contribution to make to economic development, however, it may play a significant but double-edged role in the politics of integration. All regional integration schemes have resulted in a rather rapid increase in intraregional trade. This effect, which is generally perceived as a significant benefit by the member countries, may provide an incentive for further steps toward integration, particularly since other visible benefits are not likely in the short term. However, given the tendency for these gains in trade to be distributed unequally, and to increase the role of foreign investment, the ultimate effect of trade liberalization may in the long run be to undermine the basis for cooperation in taking further steps toward integration. These further steps may include joint projects to develop a regional infrastructure or regional planning and sectoral programming, both of which are more likely to make a greater contribution to development and require greater political coordination than liberalization of trade.

Intraregional disparities, and the tendency for economic integration to reinforce them, necessitate explicit policies designed to effect more equal distribution of benefits. These policies may involve a simple transfer among member countries or an allocation of productive activity among the territories of the region. In either case, they call for a direct intervention into the economic forces operating in the region, a political action that requires agreement among the member governments beyond simply eliminating obstacles to trade.

The same is true with regard to regional policies aimed at increasing the role of local production in the regional economy through policies designed to regulate foreign investment and the transfer of technology, as in Decision 24 of the Andean Group or the Draft Agreement on Foreign Investment and Development of Technology, which CARI-COM failed to adopt. The complex nature of the policies required to respond to the complex problems of development, the rather high administrative and institutional requirements for implementing them, the controversial nature of the matters they deal with, and the perceived threat they pose to some of the established interests of the region create formidable political obstacles to their adoption and implementation. The situation is even further complicated by the tendency on the part of member governments to perceive national development gains relative to the gains of regional partners rather than in absolute terms.

The paradox of regional integration among developing countries lies in the fact that the kinds of policies most likely to contribute ultimately to development are the most difficult to adopt and implement. A clear example is sectoral programming, a policy that creates net benefits for the region by expanding productive capacity, permits equitable distribution of benefits by allocating production among member countries, and contributes to reduction of dependence by providing a defined role for local participation. Precisely because it affects these crucial questions, it raises such issues as intraregional distribution of benefits, *laissez-faire* economics versus *dirigisme*, multinational versus national companies, and the influence of metropolitan countries in the region. Yet, inasmuch as sectoral programming represents an attempt at more intensive integration on a less extensive scale, it provides a basis for political compromise. Negotiations can take place and compromises may be struck over the principal issues within a limited sector, thus allowing the perceived opportunity costs to be clearly defined and trade-offs to be made.

On a broader scale, regional development planning offers a context into which sectoral programming can be integrated. Fraught with greater political difficulties because of their broader scope, regional integration schemes have yet to move to this stage, although CARICOM has been studying the possibility of doing so for a number of years. This is one area in which the rationalization of regional production could be combined with economies of scale in the use of one scarce resource—administrative skill.

These aspects of regional integration among developing countries illustrate the extent to which the process has moved away from the *laissez-faire* approach of freeing trade toward a framework for the formulation and implementation of regional policies to restructure the existing economic relationships among member countries and with the rest of the world. Chapter 3 provides a detailed analysis of the process of Caribbean integration, which focuses on negotiations among the member countries as a function of specific integrative measures. This analysis is organized around a framework based on the principles elaborated earlier in the present section.[21]

Analysis of the Politics of Integration

Given the important differences between industrialized countries and underdeveloped countries, the politics of integration is likely to follow different patterns in the two contexts. Regional economic integration among developing countries is primarily a means by which economic development is pursued. The consequences of integration are thus evaluated on the basis of their contribution to development rather than on the basis of increased efficiency. This difference modifies the traditional criterion by which the success of integration is measured in terms of the net amount of trade creation over trade diversion, and turns all issues of integration into highly charged political questions.

Regional integration aims not at the intensification of existing economic patterns through the elimination of barriers but, rather, at a restructuring of economic patterns through the adoption of regional policies. It is through this redefinition of relationships among member countries and between the region and the metropolitan countries that regional integration takes the form of collective self-reliance. To bring about the restructuring of economic patterns, and to counter the effects of polarization within the region, "positive" measures must be adopted, thus implying a *dirigiste* rather than a *laissez-faire* approach to integration and requiring an advanced degree of political cooperation among member countries.

Attempts to establish "partial" integration schemes in the absence of measures to counter polarization and dependence are not likely to contribute to balanced regional development; they are therefore also prone to instability and likely to fail for lack of unanimous support from member countries.

We can conclude the following, then:

1. Integration schemes that are not comprehensive and *dirigiste* are more likely to stagnate than to progress.
2. The creation of a comprehensive and *dirigiste* integration scheme among developing countries is extremely difficult given the high degree of political cooperation required among countries subject to significant nationalistic forces.
3. We can identify a series of integrative measures that define different stages of the integration process, each of which provides a focus for negotiations among member countries. These negotiations in turn provide the basis for analyzing the politics of regional integration.

These conclusions direct our attention to a series of key issues in the integration process and to the negotiating positions taken on these issues by the principal actors. The level of analysis is subregional inasmuch as the politics of integration is a function of each participant's perception of the opportunity costs of participating in a regional integration scheme comprising particular "integrative measures." Integrative measures can be classified as expansive measures or distributive measures, according to whether they create benefits for the region as a whole or whether they provide for a specific distribution of benefits among member countries.[22] The more economically advanced members of an integration scheme will be more supportive of purely expansive measures because they will reap the greater share of regional gains, whereas the less advanced will be reluctant to support measures that do not have a distributive element.

Among the specific measures typically adopted by integration schemes, freeing trade and adopting a common external tariff are expansive measures in that they are directed toward providing benefits for the region as a whole and do not attempt to distribute these benefits equitably among member countries. Distributive measures, on the other hand, specifically provide for distribution of gains among member countries and typically include direct transfers from the more developed to the less developed member countries (compensatory measures), or provide for a favored treatment of the less advanced members in capital investments through development banks, investment corporations, or allocation of industries (corrective measures). Regional development planning and sectoral programming on a regional scale are especially important integrative strategies because they provide a framework in which distributive and expansive elements can be united in a compromise package that is likely to gain support from all members of an integration scheme. Because such strategies require agreement on a comprehensive basis, however, they are difficult to achieve.

In the analysis of the process of Caribbean integration that follows, emphasis is placed on the issues of creation of gains from integration, distribution of those gains, and reduction of dependence on metropolitan countries.[23] Regional policies in the agricultural sector are analyzed as elements of the overall process of integration, which revolves around the question of gains in industrialization. Seen from this perspective, the original steps in regional agricultural policy—that is, the Agricultural Marketing Protocol (AMP) and Guaranteed Market Scheme (GMS)—were perceived as distributive elements providing benefits for the less advanced member countries, which were less likely to receive significant gains in the industrial sector. In subsequent chapters, regional agricultural policy in CARICOM will be examined in detail against the background of agricultural conditions in the Caribbean.

Notes

1. Food and Agriculture Organization (FAO), *Agriculture in Regional Integration: Report of a Discussion of Comparative Experiences in Practical Aspects of Integrating National Agricultures,* seminar on Agriculture in Regional Integration (Rome: FAO, 1976), p. 1. An earlier discussion of agriculture in integration is found in Montague Yudelman and Frederic Howard, *Agricultural Development and Economic Integration in Latin America* (London: Allen & Unwin, 1970). In this latter study, Yudelman and Howard suggest a parallel integration in industry and agriculture.

2. FAO, *Agriculture in Regional Integration,* p. 1.

3. José Garrido Rojas, "Consideraciones sobre agricultura y la ALALC," in José Garrido Rojas, ed., *La agricultura en la integración latinoamericana* (Santiago: Universidad de Chile, 1977), pp. 22–23.

4. Carlos A. Wirth, "La agricultura y la integración económica en los Paises de la ALALC," documento presentado para el Seminario de Integración

Agricola (Washington, D.C.: Banco Interamericano de Desarrollo, Asesoria de Integración), pp. 21–22.

5. See FAO, *Agriculture in Regional Integration,* Appendix 4, p. iii. See also Raymundo Barros Charlin, "El Marco Jurídico de la Integración Agricola," in Rojas, *La agricultura en integración latinoamericana,* pp. 48–52.

6. Interamerican Development Bank (IDB), "Considerations on Agricultural Trade and Development in the Economic Integration of Latin America," document submitted by the IDB for the Seminar on Agricultural Integration (Washington, D.C.: IDB, 1971), pp. 6–7.

7. FAO, *Agriculture in Regional Integration,* Appendix 4, p. i.

8. Ibid., Appendix 4, p. ii.

9. Charlin, "El Marco Jurídico de la Integración Agricola," p. 59.

10. FAO, *Agriculture in Regional Integration,* Appendix 4, p. iii.

11. Charlin, "El Marco Jurídico de la Integración Agricola," p. 60.

12. Rojas, "Consideraciones sobre agricultura y la ALALC," p. 29.

13. FAO, *Agriculture in Regional Integration,* Appendix 4, p. iii. The major steps implementing regional agricultural policy in the Andean Group include Decision 16 (1970), Decision 43 (1971), Decision 76 (1976), and Decisions 92 and 93 (1975).

14. Ibid., pp. vi–x. Examples of integration schemes with agricultural provisions include the Agreements on Arab Economic Unity, the Arab Common Market, the Maghreb Integration Scheme, Regional Cooperation for Development (RCD), the West Africa Economic Community (CEAO), the Economic Community of West African States (ECOWAS), and the Association of South East Asian Nations (ASEAN). The East African Community (EAC) and the Union Douanière des Etats d'Afrique Centrale (UDEAC) provided for no special measures in the agricultural sector.

15. A more complete discussion of these ideas can be found in W. Andrew Axline, "Latin American Regional Integration: Alternative Perspectives on a Changing Reality," *Latin American Research Review* 6 (Spring 1981):167–186.

16. This criterion is found in Jacob Viner, *The Customs Union Issue* (New York: Carnegie Endowment for International Peace, 1950), and in virtually all expositions of traditional customs union theory. See J. F. Meade, *Problems of Economic Union* (Chicago: University of Chicago Press, 1953), and *The Theory of Customs Union* (Amsterdam: North Holland Publishing Company, 1955); Rolf Stanwald and Jacques Stohler, *Economic Integration* (Princeton, N.J.: Princeton University Press, 1959); Tibor Scitovsky, *Economic Theory and Western European Integration* (Stanford, Calif.: Stanford University Press, 1958); Jan Tinbergen, *International Economic Integration* (Amsterdam: Elsevier, 1954); Bela Balassa, *The Theory of Economic Integration* (Homewood, Ill.: Richard D. Irwin, 1961).

17. Hiroshi Kitamura, "Economic Theory and the Integration of Underdeveloped Regions," in Miguel S. Wionczek, ed., *Latin American Economic Integration* (New York: Praeger Publishers, 1966); Raymond F. Mikesell, "The Theory of Common Markets as Applied to Regional Arrangements Among

Developing Countries," in Roy Harrod and Douglas Hague, eds., *International Trade Theory in a Developing World* (New York: St. Martin's Press, 1963); Tayseer Jaber, "The Relevance of Traditional Integration Theory to Less Developed Countries," *Journal of Common Market Studies* 11 (March 1971); R. S. Bhambri, "Customs Unions and Under-Developed Countries," *Economia internazionale* 15 (May 1962); F. Kahnert et al., *Economic Integration among Developing Countries* (Paris: OECD, 1969); Fuat Andic, Suphan Andic, and Douglas Dosser, *A Theory of Economic Integration for Developing Countries* (London: Allen & Unwin, 1971); Jorge Sakamoto, "Industrial Development and Integration of Underdeveloped Countries," *Journal of Common Market Studies* 7 (June 1969); Bela Balassa, *Economic Development and Integration* (Mexico: Grafica Panamericana, 1965); Yu-Min Chou, "Economic Integration in Less Developed Countries," *Journal of Development Studies* (July 1971); C. A. Cooper and B. Massell, "Toward a General Theory of Customs Unions for Developing Countries," *Journal of Political Economy* 73 (1965).

18. W. Arthur Lewis, "The Industrialization of the British West Indies," *Caribbean Economic Review* (May 1950); Raúl Prebisch, *The Economic Development of Latin America and Its Principal Problems* (New York: United Nations, 1950).

19. Latin American integration has been criticized on this basis by Susanne Bodenheimer in "Masterminding the Mini-Market: U.S. Aid to the Central American Common Market," *NACLA Report* (May 1973), and Bodenheimer, "Dependency and Imperialism: The Roots of Latin American Underdevelopment," in K. T. Fann and Donald C. Hodges, eds., *Readings in U.S. Imperialism* (Boston: Porter Sargent, 1971), p. 167; André Gunder Frank, "Latin American Economic Integration," in André Gunder Frank, ed., *Latin America: Underdevelopment or Revolution* (New York: Monthly Review Press, 1969), pp. 175–180; Havelock Brewster and Clive Y. Thomas, *The Dynamics of West Indian Economic Integration* (Mona, Jamaica: Institute for Social and Economic Research [ISER], 1967); Clive Y. Thomas, "Neo-Colonialism and Caribbean Integration," *Ratoon* (April 1975):1–28.

20. This evolution is presaged in Constantine V. Vaitsos, "Crisis in Regional Economic Cooperation (Integration) Among Developing Countries," *World Development* (1978).

21. A formal presentation of the theoretical principles on which this general discussion is based is found in W. Andrew Axline, "Underdevelopment, Dependence and Integration: The Politics of Regionalism in the Third World," *International Organization* 31 (Winter 1977):83–105.

22. The theoretical basis for this distinction is found in Barbara Haskel, "Disparities, Strategies, and Opportunity Costs: The Example of Scandinavian Economic Market Negotiations," *International Studies Quarterly* 18 (March 1974):3–30.

23. A detailed analysis of Caribbean integration within this framework is found in W. Andrew Axline, *Caribbean Integration: The Politics of Regionalism* (London: Frances Pinter; New York: Nichols Publishing, 1979). A good political history of CARIFTA/CARICOM is also provided by Anthony Payne, *The Politics of the Caribbean Community 1961–1979* (Manchester: University of Manchester Press, 1980).

3
The Process of
Caribbean Integration

Although the general principles relating to integration among developing countries presented in the preceding chapter are not meant to describe a chronological process, Caribbean integration did evolve along those general lines. This evolution reflects both a learning process derived from the integration experience and a situation of ideological ferment within the region. We can look at this evolution of CARIFTA and CARICOM within the overall context of the region, describe its elements within the framework already elaborated, and study the impact of political events on the integration process.[1]

The Negotiations for Caribbean Integration

The negotiations for Caribbean integration reflect a pattern that closely parallels the theoretical conception of Third World integration outlined in Chapter 2. Three principal stages describe the integrative process. The first, which set the pattern for later negotiations, was the original decision in 1967-1968 to establish an integration scheme in the form of a free trade area, CARIFTA. The second and most important stage was the creation in 1973 of the customs union that eventually became CARICOM. In this period the dominant pattern of negotiating positions clearly emerged. The third stage was the refusal by the heads of government in 1974 to adopt a common policy to control foreign investment, thus demonstrating the limits to regional integration in the Caribbean.

The discussion and negotiations for the establishment of CARIFTA took place in two steps. The first centered on conference of Caribbean government officials in Georgetown, Guyana, in August 1967. The second began at the Heads of Government Conference in October 1967 with the adoption of the proposals of the August meeting, and was concluded in August 1968 when all members had adhered to the CARIFTA Agreement.[2]

UK

laissez faire
vs
dirigiste
(market vs
c
marxist)

Spurred by the United Kingdom's application to enter the European Economic Community and by the signing of an agreement by Antigua, Barbados, and Guyana, officials of the region met in August 1967 to establish a region-wide free trade area. The discussions at this meeting focused on two distinct approaches to integration: a *laissez-faire* approach adopted by the business community of the region (the ICCC)[3] in their proposal for "phased freeing of trade,"[4] and a *dirigiste* approach propounded by scholars from the University of the West Indies in a series of studies commissioned by the governments of the region, which advocated the "integration of production."[5]

The proposals adopted by the 1967 conference reflect the "phased freeing of trade" approach. Central was a resolution (which became effective on May 1, 1968) to eliminate all import duties and quantitative restrictions of products traded among Commonwealth Caribbean countries. A reserve list of certain products to be exempted from free trade for five years (eight years for the LDCs) was established, and nondiscriminatory fiscal measures were permitted to offset customs revenue losses.[6] A separate resolution called for the establishment of a Caribbean Development Bank along the lines that had been suggested in a report by the United Nations Development Program (UNDP).[7]

"for consideration"
= dreams

Beyond these proposals, the conference called for "consideration" of a number of other measures that might eventually be adopted as part of the integration scheme. These measures provided a long-term "agenda" for Caribbean integration and served as a basis for subsequent Secretariat initiatives, including creation of the customs union that became CARICOM. The list of measures was adopted as Annex A to the CARIFTA Agreement, and it included a common external tariff and common regime of quantitative restrictions, the harmonization of fiscal incentives and establishment of regional industries, measures to ensure allocation of industries to the LDCs, the establishment of regional integrated industry, and the establishment of regional agricultural marketing.[8]

The proposals of the Georgetown Conference were accepted at the October 1967 Heads of Government Conference, but when CARIFTA came into being on May 1, 1968, only four states had signed the agreement, with Trinidad and Tobago joining the original three countries of Antigua, Barbados, and Guyana. The LDCs were dissatisfied because of the lack of distributive measures, and they remained outside while forming their own subregional customs union—namely, the East Caribbean Common Market (ECCM). Jamaica, still wary of regional political integration from its earlier experience in the West Indies Federation, and unsure of its competitive position in regional trade vis-à-vis Trinidad and Tobago, also hesitated. The period from

ECCM

May until August 1968, during which all members joined, marks the beginning of the pattern of negotiations in Caribbean integration.

For the MDCs, the essentially expansive nature of CARIFTA meant that they would reap the larger part of the regional gains. The LDCs perceived that the absence of effective distributive mechanisms would result in economic losses, certainly relative to the MDCs and possibly in an absolute sense as well. Jamaica's reluctance to participate for fear of having to forgo or transfer regional gains confirmed in the eyes of the LDCs the unwillingness of the MDCs to share regional benefits equitably. These conflicting interests were dramatized in a dispute over the site of the Caribbean Development Bank (CDB). The proposal to locate the bank in St. Vincent, as a symbol of the need to provide benefits to the LDCs, was vehemently opposed by Jamaica, whose government made the location of the bank in Jamaica a condition for its participation in CARIFTA. After a number of stormy sessions, the other member governments agreed on Barbados as a compromise site, which Jamaica eventually accepted. On August 1, 1968, Jamaica and Montserrat joined CARIFTA, the other ECCM countries having signed on July 1. The present membership was completed when Belize formally joined as the eighth LDC on May 1, 1971.

Although the conception of regional integration that emerged in the resolutions of the 1967 Georgetown Conference was a comprehensive one, during its first five years of operations CARIFTA essentially constituted a *laissez-faire* integration scheme involving the elimination of tariffs and quantitative restrictions on intraregional trade. According to the Commonwealth Caribbean Regional Secretariat, from the very beginning some 90 percent of intraregional trade was freed.[9] The essentially expansive nature of CARIFTA was further confirmed in the statement made by ECLA's office for the Caribbean in Port of Spain:

> Since its inception the CARIFTA has been regarded as a process for accelerating trade between its members and stimulating production, although other aspects of regional integration might be considered equally important. At the end of 1972 it is still essentially a Free Trade Area, and progress must be assessed primarily in terms of the acceleration of intra-area trade.[10]

Costs of participation for the LDCs were reduced somewhat by means of the reserve list and less stringent application of some of the other obligations, but the limited integration scheme that had been negotiated in 1968 was unrealized, and the LDCs were faced with certain costs for their integration while its benefits remained largely in the realm of promises.

The agreement establishing the Caribbean Development Bank was not signed until October 19, 1969, and the bank itself was not formally established until January 1970. Even after its formal establishment, it failed to live up to the expectations held by the LDCs, which had envisioned it to be a major corrective mechanism. In 1970 one project for hotel development was approved,[11] and in 1971 twenty projects totaling approximately EC$6 million were approved.[12] The CDB, however, was hampered by lengthy loan procedures. As in any under-developed region, administrative skills were in short supply. Applications for funds were (and still are) required to satisfy the stringent criteria that often fall beyond the capacity of the applicants most in need of development capital. Moreover, as the CDB could finance only a part of the funds, the applicant had to find other sources of finance—not only a difficult task but also one usually predicated on the credit rating the applicant receives when the CDB awards its loan. Together these factors explain the long delays that occurred between approval of the request and actual payment of funds. In 1972, for example, funds for projects totaling EC$6 million were approved whereas approximately EC$500,000 were paid out.[13]

The cumbersome nature of procuring loans, which entails rigorous lending criteria, was due in part to the CDB's operation on a regional scale as a type of International Bank for Reconstruction and Development (IBRD) rather than as an integration bank whose major purpose was to serve as a corrective measure. Partial steps were taken to correct this situation by the MDCs, who agreed to leave the "soft loan" funds entirely to the LDCs. Later, William Demas, successor to Sir Arthur Lewis as president of the Caribbean Development Bank, adopted a conception of the institution that falls more along the lines of an integration bank.[14]

During the time in which the LDCs were experiencing frustration over the ineffectiveness of the CDB, the gains from liberalizing trade were primarily benefiting the MDCs. From 1967 to 1971, total CARIFTA intraregional imports rose from EC$95 million to an estimated EC$188 million—an increase of 98 percent for the period, or an average of 19 percent per year. Prior to CARIFTA, the average annual growth rate was less than 6 percent per year.[15] The growth of intraregional trade continued rising to EC$260 million for 1972, EC$298 million for 1973,[16] and EC$510 million in 1974.[17]

Trade among the MDCs, Barbados, Guyana, Jamaica, and the republic of Trinidad and Tobago accounted for over 60 percent of the regional trade in 1967 and 69 percent in 1971. During this same period, intra-area trade between the LDCs declined from 1.9 percent to 1.4 percent of the total regional trade.[18] This pattern of trade polarization was strongly felt by the LDCs and was further exacerbated by a high rate of inflation.

The Agricultural Marketing Protocol (AMP)—which was created as the basis for rationalizing agricultural production in the region, reducing dependence on imports of foodstuffs from third countries, and providing benefits for the more agricultural LDCs—also contributed to polarization within the region. The LDCs, in addition to being less industrialized, were also less competitive in agricultural production. The guaranteed minimum regional price of the Agricultural Marketing Protocol (AMP) stimulated greater production in the MDCs, thus further weakening the position of the LDCs. To offset this situation and to build real compensatory aspects into the regional agricultural system, the Guaranteed Market Scheme (GMS) was devised to provide protected access to MDC markets for agricultural products from the LDCs.[19] Yet the AMP did not respond to claims by LDCs for a share of regional development through structural transformation by creating industrial bases in their countries. The LDCs were unwilling to become the primary producers in an industrializing Caribbean region. Allocation of industries within their countries was the kind of corrective measure they sought, but the measure had remained a dead letter since its incorporation into the resolutions of the 1967 Georgetown Conference.

The acute awareness of the unequal distribution of benefits can be seen in individual and official statements of the LDC members. A Barbados trade mission touring the CARIFTA territories in 1969 found general dissatisfaction among the smaller territories, which felt that they were being dominated by the MDCs. The business community of the LDCs was found to be pessimistic, and an official of the St. Lucia Marketing Board specifically mentioned agricultural competition from Trinidad's oranges.[20] James Fitzallen Mitchell, minister of trade for St. Vincent, while admitting that the AMP had stimulated sales of sweet potatoes to Trinidad and Tobago, accused Trinidad of being unfair in trying to exploit the limited agricultural benefits of the region as well as the industrial benefits.[21]

In his address to the annual meeting in January 1970, the president of the Chamber of Commerce of Dominica made a comprehensive summary of the LDCs' position. He accused CARIFTA of having caused a sudden increase in prices through consumption taxes and profiteering by manufacturers in the four MDCs, and he declared that the LDCs had gained little and suffered considerable disadvantage from integration. He went on to point out that proposals for some allocation of industry to LDCs had not been implemented, that the people of the Associated States felt abandoned, and that for them CARIFTA was a dead loss.[22]

It was within this setting of actual and perceived polarization of gains that the next stage of negotiations was prepared. Steps were taken to implement another principle agreed upon at the 1967 Georgetown Conference: the adoption of a common external tariff. This measure was expansive rather than distributive. It would create regional economic benefits through trade diversion, in which case the benefits would be likely to reinforce the disparity between the two groups.

The move to establish a common external tariff within CARIFTA became the most contentious issue of the Caribbean integration movement. The period from 1971 to 1973 took on the characteristics of a permanent crisis until agreement was finally reached on a linked expansive-distributive policy, which created a package of integrative measures acceptable to all members.

Pursuant to the commitment to study the feasibility of a common external tariff (CET) in the 1967 resolution, the CARIFTA Council of Ministers in 1970 appointed a committee under the leadership of Secretary-General William Demas. The report of this committee was distributed early in 1971 to the members,[23] who adopted positions on the tariff issue. The MDCs strongly supported the CET, Jamaica's position evolved from reluctance to acceptance, and the LDCs showed great resistance to it.

As in 1968, Trinidad and Tobago and Guyana were the most eager of all the territories in the region to deepen the integration movement. In 1970, Trinidad and Tobago expressed the hope that a CET would be adopted by early 1972.[24] Earlier in the same year, Guyana's prime minister, Forbes Burnham, asked for the harmonization of fiscal incentives and a common external tariff.[25] His support provided a favorable political base for the Secretariat's efforts to move to the next stage of integration. Barbados, seeking a protected regional market for its fledgling light industry, supported the idea, although its relatively low national tariff meant that prices would probably increase. In Barbados, as in Jamaica, the eventual support for the CET reflected a policy advocated by the manufacturing sector as opposed to commercial interests—a division that also existed in the regional business organization known as the Caribbean Association of Industry and Commerce (CAIC).[26]

Jamaica was the only country in which a major internal debate took place. The Jamaican position evolved to one of support from the earlier 1968 position expressed by that country's high commissioner in Trinidad: "Participation (in CARIFTA) would be in respect of a free trade agreement within the Caribbean area and not in a Common Market involving uniformity of external tariffs or full economic integration involving the first two aspects plus free movement of peoples among other important factors."[27]

In 1972, however, the Jamaican prime minister, Michael Manley, declared that the harmonization of fiscal incentives and the establishment of a common external tariff were very important steps that proceeded from the existence of CARIFTA.[28] This shift in policy followed a change of government in 1972 and reflected the ambivalence of Jamaica's policy toward CARIFTA during this period. Such ambivalence flowed, on the one hand, from the contradiction between the trade increases and the potential benefits to manufacturing that Jamaica had gained from a protected regional market and, on the other, from the continuing fear of being involved in a regional political union that might necessitate the sacrifice of possible bilateral arrangements with the United States, the United Kingdom, and Canada.

Robert Lightbourne, Jamaican minister of trade and leader of a CARIFTA mission to Europe and Great Britain in 1969, specifically referred to the Jamaican referendum on federation in stating his objection to any political content in CARIFTA's objectives. He cited the alternative possibility of integration with the United States, Canada, or even England.[29] Later, as an independent member of Parliament, Lightbourne said of Caribbean integration that it "appears to be growing into a federation in everything but name."[30] Jamaica's new government, however, was in favor of a CET, which the private sector also supported. The Jamaican government's shift in agreeing to further integration was a key element in permitting the eventual establishment of CARICOM.

Meanwhile, the LDCs were coalescing around a position opposed to the tariff. They saw the adoption of a common external tariff as a move that would exacerbate the unfavorable situation that had resulted from the creation of CARIFTA. At the ninth Council of Ministers' meeting in 1971, the LDCs strongly voiced their resistance to the CET.[31] While expressing their support for the principle of further integration, they stated that the new tariff would lead to further socioeconomic problems in the countries that depended heavily on customs for public revenue.[32] The government of Dominica argued that the tariff would create artificial barriers leading to higher prices and lower quality.[33] The government of Montserrat, which was to become the most outspoken of the LDCs, stated that since the country was not benefiting from CARIFTA, it would never agree to the harmonization of fiscal incentives or to a CET.[34]

From the beginning of the October 1972 meeting in Trinidad, the deadlock between the MDCs and the LDCs was apparent. At the council meeting immediately preceding the Heads of Government Conference, the LDCs made it clear that they were not prepared to take further steps toward deepening integration unless the MDCs were committed to making a "tangible manifestation of the ways in which development is going to come to the Less Developed Countries."[35]

The MDCs proposed a number of "opting out" mechanisms rather than ensuring the LDCs a greater share of the benefits of integration. Although these proposed measures would have lowered the short-term costs of participation for the LDCs, presumably until some benefits of industrialization had been realized, they did not satisfy demands for the concrete steps needed to allocate industries to the LDCs. The measure finally taken to address this issue—the creation of the Caribbean Investment Corporation—originated not from a proposal made by one of the member governments but from a joint effort of the CARIFTA Secretariat and the Caribbean Association of Industry and Commerce (CAIC), which approached the LDCs in September 1972 hoping to find a compromise permitting the adoption of a common external tariff.

The question of allocation of industries had been included in Annex A of CARIFTA, along with the CET and the harmonization of fiscal incentives. Indeed, allocation of industries within the region was perhaps the most carefully examined of all the principles involved in the deepening of regional integration. At the tenth Council of Ministers' meeting, the member governments passed a resolution establishing the Location of Industry Task Force headed by Secretary-General William Demas. The task force viewed the promotion of industrial development in the LDCs as an end in itself and as a means of achieving a more equitable distribution of benefits within CARIFTA. The LDCs' insistence on a distributive policy resulted in the proposal of a corrective measure designed to increase their opportunities for industrialization. Specifically, the measure proposed the establishment of a regional investment company that would provide equity capital for the establishment of industry in the LDCs.

The Caribbean Association of Industry and Commerce (CAIC) report contained six recommendations, the last of which provided the basis for the ultimate compromise on the creation of CARICOM.[36] It recommended that "an intensive study of the feasibility of an Investment Company as conceived and developed in discussions with both the Public and Private Sectors during the tour should be vigorously pursued by the CARIFTA Secretariat." This item, added after the other recommendations had been drafted, was the key element in the package of measures agreed upon at the seventh Heads of Government Conference as the basis for moving from CARIFTA to CARICOM. An agreement on a common approach to negotiations between the Caribbean governments and the European Economic Community was ratified, and the final communiqué of the conference included the major points of the initial proposal. It was agreed that the Caribbean Free Trade Association would become the Caribbean Common Market on May 1, 1973, and that there would be a series of measures designed to promote the economic development of the LDCs, particularly their industrial development. There were proposals for the harmonization of fiscal incentives, the establishment of a common external tariff, a common protective policy, rationalization of agriculture, greater monetary and financial cooperation, and measures for location of industry in the LDCs. Accepted were proposals for the establishment of a Caribbean multinational investment company, an export credit insurance scheme to be operated by the Caribbean Development Bank, private and public technical assistance, and the use of technical research facilities in the MDCs by the LDCs.[37]

These proposals, along with the amendments to Articles 5, 17, 18, and 39 of the CARIFTA Agreement, defined the nature of the new Caribbean integration scheme to be adopted. Between October 1972 and the eighth Heads of Government Conference in Georgetown, Guyana, in April 1973, however, details of the package had to be worked out. Final negotiations were to be settled at the thirteenth Council of Ministers' meeting immediately preceding the eighth Heads of Government Conference, at which the agreement would be ratified.

Rather than being a simple exercise in ironing out the final points of negotiation over the compromise to be ratified by the Heads of Government Conference, however, the Council of Ministers found itself deadlocked in the first day of its meeting, when the government of Montserrat placed a "surprise" document before the council demanding specific distributive concessions from the MCDs. The "Montserrat paper," as the document came to be called, contained a comprehensive statement of the need for "positive"—or *dirigiste*—mechanisms, including the direct transfer of funds from the MDCs to the LDCs.[38] Although the document was submitted by the government of Montserrat, it had been prepared in collaboration with the East Caribbean Common Market (ECCM) Secretariat and thus represented a broader LDC position. It began with a survey of the problems and prospects of Caribbean integration, including a sophisticated analysis of the nature and causes of polarization and criticism of existing measures to counter the problem.

The Government of Montserrat is not persuaded that current regional economic integration programmes proposed for the Commonwealth Caribbean give anything like adequate recognition to the dangers of polarization in the Commonwealth Caribbean context. It is simply not credible that the proposed amendments to the CARIFTA Agreement, the harmonization of fiscal incentives to industry, the establishment of a Caribbean Investment Corporation and the activities of the Caribbean Development Bank will, by themselves, arrest, let alone reverse, current trends toward polarization.[39]

Following an extensive analysis was a series of twelve proposals for action to be taken in order to realize the long-term aspirations of integration.[40] The paper concluded with the request that Montserrat be accorded a special position among the LDCs analogous to Barbados's position among the MDCs, with concessionary measures being applied for its benefit.[41]

The discussion of the Montserrat paper and related questions of the distribution of benefits from integration occupied virtually all the discussion at the thirteenth council meeting, which ended in a deadlock after five days of deliberation. The issues carried over into the eighth Heads of Government Conference, with a sharp division still existing between MDCs and LDCs and with some delegates threatening to create a common market without the LDCs.[42] One delegate was quoted as saying of the LDCs that "they want to see the smoke coming from the factories before signing the agreement for the common market."[43] Attributed to a Jamaican delegate was the comment that "the man who coined the term *MDCs* should be assassinated."[44]

These statements provide a clear expression of the tension between nationalist forces and the requirements of regionalism. However, on the basis of the existing proposals, and given the realization that a crucial stage in the development of Caribbean integration was at hand, the member countries arrived at a compromise permitting the establishment of the Caribbean Common Market and Community.

The key element in this compromise, embodied in the Georgetown Accord signed on April 12, 1973, was the creation of the Caribbean Investment Corporation (CIC), which was intended to provide equity investment in projects in the LDCs with 60 percent of the funds subscribed from the member governments and 40 percent from the private sector. It did not satisfy the demands of the LDCs for direct allocation of industry, but it did constitute a genuine corrective measure and represented the maximum concession that the MDCs would give in exchange for the expansive measure of the common external tariff. The LDCs had no choice but to accept it.

The Georgetown Accord provided for the creation of a customs union and for the initiation on June 1, 1973, of three agreements of special interest to the LDCs: the Agreement on the Harmonization of Fiscal Incentives to Industry, the Agreement on the Avoidance of Double Taxation, and the Agreement on the Establishment of the Caribbean Investment Corporation, as well as other special measures allowing the LDCs to be exempted from the rules of the Common Market.[45] Montserrat was given special consideration among the LDCs. In effect, the Georgetown Accord was an agreement to proceed to CARICOM in two stages, with the MDCs joining in August 1973 and the LDCs joining in May 1974.

The MDCs signed the Treaty of Chaguaramas establishing CARICOM on July 4, 1973. In April 1974, Grenada, Belize, Dominica, Montserrat, St. Vincent, and St. Lucia adhered. On July 26, 1974, St. Kitts-Nevis, which had been constitutionally blocked from signing over the question of Anguilla, became the final member to join the Caribbean Community and Common Market. At that time, Caribbean integration moved to a customs union combined with a series of other measures to establish a more advanced type of integration scheme based on an expansive-distributive package.

The Caribbean Development Bank had been the principal distributive element in the CARIFTA negotiations. Unfortunately, just as there had been disappointment with the CDB, the CIC failed to satisfy the demands of the LDCs for measures that would allocate industrial production to them. In the first two years of CIC's operation, the private sector fell far short in its subscription of shares; even though the governments of the region paid their share immediately, the CIC required some time before projects could be funded. Thus, with the LDCs still dissatisfied, the third stage of negotiations in Caribbean integration began with the proposal to adopt a regional policy to regulate foreign investment.

At the eighth Heads of Government Conference in 1973, a working party was created to study the question of foreign investment in the region, a matter that was not on the "agenda" of Annex A of the CARIFTA Agreement but one that had been the subject of study by the CARIFTA Secretariat and academics of the region and had been raised a number of times by the government of Guyana.[46] Owing to the contentious nature of the issue, the working party carried out its work in great secrecy, and intergovernmental discussion of controlling foreign investment in the region excluded all but the highest officials. Drawing on the experiences of a number of countries that had adopted policies of regulating foreign investment and transferring technology— particularly Mexico, the republic of Trinidad and Tobago, and the

Andean Group's Decision 24—and after drafting several protocols, the working party proposed a Draft Agreement on Foreign Investment and Development of Technology for adoption at the July 1974 Heads of Government Conference in St. Lucia. But before the Draft Agreement could be discussed in any detail, the LDCs expressed their adamant opposition to it, thus effectively blocking a common regional policy on foreign investment. All of the MDCs were willing to accept the proposal, with Guyana and Trinidad as its major proponents. On this issue, however, there was no compromise between the LDCs and the MDCs, and the Draft Agreement was referred back to the working party for further study.[47]

The Draft Agreement can be seen as an expansive measure in that it provided for a reduction of foreign control of key sectors of the regional economy and for the development of a more indigenous technology. It represented a logical extension of the regime for the harmonization of fiscal incentives at no new cost to the MDCs, which had received the major portion of foreign investment in the region. However, the LDCs, still anxious to pursue foreign investment under any conditions, opposed what they perceived as a deterrent to it and, hence, also as a hindrance to their eventual industrialization. To satisfy their needs they required an expansive measure, which in turn required a corresponding distributive measure in the form of guaranteed investment. Lacking this expansive-distributive policy compromise, CARICOM failed to move to an integration scheme with an effective policy to reduce dependence.[48] But this is not to suggest that Caribbean integration has stagnated to the same degree that LAFTA has. Although the eventual adoption of measures to reduce dependence will be necessary if integration is to make a major contribution to the development of the region, in the period since the rejection of the Draft Agreement CARICOM has pursued other measures to consolidate the customs union and existing distributive measures. Nonetheless, the ability of CARICOM to progress in a way that will contribute to the development of the region is limited by the constraints of dependence and the tendency to pursue nationalistic rather than regional solutions to immediate economic problems. The activities of CARICOM since its failure to adopt a regional regime to control foreign investment illustrate these contradictory pulls.

The State of Caribbean Integration

The failure to adopt a regime to control foreign investment does not signal the end of Caribbean integration, although it does indicate the limits beyond which it is not prepared to go. The integration process continues, though without moving to the next stage suggested by the theoretical framework outlined in Chapter 2. CARICOM has continued to function since 1974 within the constraints imposed both by the failure to take this important step and by existing intraregional and international political and economic influences.

The period subsequent to the 1974 decision on the Draft Agreement demonstrates the contradiction between attempts to maintain a regional integration scheme based on the phased freeing of trade within the twin constraints of an international economic crisis on the one hand and particularistic tendencies within the region on the other hand. The result was that by mid-1978 Caribbean integration was in disarray, what with the imposition of import restrictions by two of the four MDCs; the shelving of plans for the joint smelter project among the republic of Trinidad and Tobago, Guyana, and Jamaica; and the pursuit of bilateral arrangements with third countries by a number of CARICOM members at the expense of regional cooperation.

During the same period, however, other events were occurring that reinforced the established pattern of regional negotiations and indicated a tendency to move toward a more *dirigiste* form of integration. The worldwide economic crisis in 1974 further strained the Caribbean integration movement. Integrative measures that involved difficult economic and political choices faced even greater obstacles during this period. The inflation that had begun in 1972 continued to accelerate, and was combined with an energy crisis that saw a fourfold increase in the price of oil and a food crisis that resulted in a rapidly growing regional food import bill.

The republic of Trinidad and Tobago, as a petroleum-exporting country, has been less hard hit by these crises; but as a very small producer (given an annual output of less than 0.5 percent of total world production), it has not benefited as the major world oil producers have. The other MDCs suffered recurrent budgetary and balance-of-payments deficits over the period 1974–1977, even though inflation had slowed somewhat. And even in the case of Trinidad and Tobago, the visible trade deficit (excluding oil) had increased sharply by 1976. The region's two bauxite and alumina exporters, Guyana and Jamaica, were able to increase revenues from this source by nationalizing and increasing levies. But in spite of these levies, both countries experienced increasing budgetary and balance-of-payments deficits. In 1977 both Guyana and Jamaica resorted to import restrictions, and in May 1978 Jamaica was forced to undertake another in a series of devaluations as a condition of obtaining IMF balance-of-payments support. In addition, economic conditions were exacerbated by numerous instances of industrial unrest, including damaging strikes in the oil industry of Trinidad and Tobago in 1976 and in the sugar industry in Guyana in 1977.

The LDCs were the hardest hit of all. Consumer and other import prices increased dramatically, and their primary exports were subject to the usual unstable conditions. Sugar, which had reached a price of £650 (US$1,892) in the world market toward the end of 1974, declined rapidly to about £160 (US$463) a ton, and in 1977 the cost of production in some countries was higher than the price negotiated with the European Community under the Lomé Convention. In addition, bananas, citrus fruits, and spices were subject to unfavorable market conditions. All of the LDCs faced varying degrees of fiscal crisis with significant budget deficits on current account, and the governments announced a number of tax measures and expenditure cuts in order to reduce the deficits. Tourism also suffered, mainly because of the inflation in North America, which was the major source of tourists to the area, but also because of perceived social unrest in the region.

Economic conditions in the area remained depressed into the early 1980s partly as a result of slow growth, inflation, and restrictive fiscal and monetary policies in the OECD countries and partly as a result of the vulnerability of the Caribbean countries to external economic conditions. During the course of 1983 there were signs of recovery, strongest in North America and weaker in Europe and Japan. The strong growth of the U.S. economy in 1984 and into 1985, along with the continued lower rates of inflation, provided some optimism for improved performance among the Caribbean countries. Lower oil prices also provided the basis for some optimism for the non-oil-producing members of the region. Nonetheless, the relatively slow economic recovery among industrialized countries and the lag in the effect of OECD performance on the economic situation of developing countries led to little improvement in Caribbean economies by 1984.[49] Moreover, low international demand for commodities led to continued low prices in 1984, although the lower rate of inflation in industrialized countries provided some stability in import prices. Missing were two essential elements of long-term improvement—increases in productivity and expanded output in the major economic sectors of the region.

During the 1982-1983 crop year, sugar production fell below 1981-1982 levels (from 887,110 tons to 841,928 tons), thus continuing the decline in the industry over the past few years. Only Belize recorded an increase in output. Domestic oil production in Trinidad and Tobago has been declining since 1979, although natural gas production rose by 4 percent in the first half of 1983. Bauxite production declined by 7.2 percent in Jamaica in 1983 and 6.4 percent in Guyana compared to the previous year. On the other hand, banana production in the Windward Islands and Belize increased by 9.5 percent, and arrivals of stop-over visitors to main tourist destinations showed an upswing in 1983 and 1984.[50]

Intraregional imports in CARICOM rose from 7.5 percent of total imports in 1973 to 9.3 percent in 1981 and fell back to 8.1 percent in 1982, whereas over the same period (1973–1982) intraregional domestic exports for CARICOM rose from 10.3 percent to 11.9 percent. Although the MDCs accounted for 87 percent of intraregional domestic exports in 1982 (78 percent when oil is excluded), the LDCs have managed to increase their share by 4 percent since 1973 (15 percent when oil is excluded).[51] Growth rates for regional trade are presented in Table 3.1. The republic of Trinidad and Tobago has provided some balance-of-payments support through the central banks of the other MDCs and through a special fund of the CDB for the LDCs. Balance-of-payment figures are presented in Table 3.2. Moreover, in 1976, the United Kingdom, along with the MDCs, signed an agreement with the CDB for the establishment of the Fund for Emergency Programme Assistance and for Common Services (EC$10 million). This fund makes grants and loans to the governments of the Windward and Leeward Islands for the support of essential national programs and common services in the context of the international economic crisis.

By 1975, the distributive measures of CARICOM had begun to make an impact, and both the Caribbean Development Bank and the Caribbean Investment Corporation were actively engaged in funding projects, mainly in the LDCs. A special effort was made by the CDB in 1975 to respond to the dissatisfaction of loan applicants over the slowness of the rate of disbursement of funds, and that year US$21.9 million was disbursed—a sum over three times the total amount disbursed throughout the three preceding years. By the end of 1977, a total of US$140,318,000 had been approved and US$85,391,000 had been disbursed, representing a 52.8 percent rate of disbursement to approvals. Approximately 70 percent of total disbursements were made to the LDCs, and 96 percent of the "soft funds" totaling US$40,858,000 went to them.[52]

The Caribbean Investment Corporation (CIC), which at the end of 1976 had finished its third year of operation, experienced a similar increase in activity as it became more widely recognized as possibly the only major institutional source of risk capital available exclusively for the benefit of the LDCs. By the end of 1976, the CIC had authorized funds totaling EC$1,759,540, of which $1,411,500 had

Table 3.1

CARICOM Countries:
Total and Intraregional Trade--Average Annual Growth Rates, 1973-1982
(percentages)

	Imports		Domestic Exports		Total Exports	
	Total	Intra	Total	Intra	Total	Intra
Antigua	15.3	20.2[e]	-4.9	20.7[e]	0.8	24.9[a]
Belize	16.9	-0.8	13.8	19.4	22.7[a]	19.0
Dominica	16.6	20.8	16.0	37.8	16.5	35.0
Grenada	15.3	16.5	14.9	33.3	14.8	28.6
Montserrat	17.1	16.1	39.4	39.6	29.3	n.a
St. Kitts-Nevis	14.5	17.1	14.0	31.2[e]	13.3	31.7[a]
St. Lucia	17.6	16.0	23.7	32.4	21.7	27.0
St. Vincent	17.6	13.7	27.7	36.4	27.0	34.6
LDCs Mean	16.4	16.0[e]	18.1	30.3	15.9	27.5[e]
Barbados	18.5	19.9	21.6	24.7	23.3	23.6
Guyana	9.2	17.1	10.2	11.6	11.2	12.4
Jamaica	12.5	15.2	11.7	18.0	11.8	18.0
Trinidad & Tobago	22.9	31.1	21.9	19.9	22.1	19.5
MDCs Mean	15.8	20.7	16.4	18.6	17.1	18.4
CARICOM Mean	16.2	19.7[e]	17.5	20.1	18.5	19.8[e]

SOURCE: CARICOM Secretariat, "Patterns of Intra-regional Trade in the Caribbean Community 1973-1983," CARICOM Bulletin, no. 5 (1984), Table 9, p. 39.

[a] Data for 1973-1981.
[e] Estimated.

been disbursed. Of the authorized capital stock of the CIC, EC$5 million of the total EC$15 million was to be paid in the first issue over five years. At the end of 1976, the public sector had paid EC$2,909,995 of its $3 million share, but the private sector had paid only EC$1,272,600 of its $2 million share.[53] By 1980, the Caribbean Investment Corporation had essentially ceased to function as an effective corrective measure, but it continued to operate as a "holding operation," overseeing existing investments yet engaging in no new enterprises. In 1981, efforts were undertaken to revive the CIC, but by the end of 1982 it was clear that the institution that had been a key element in negotiating the common external tariff would not survive. In January 1983, a decision was taken to formally

Table 3.2

CARICOM Countries:
Current Account Balance of Payments, 1977-1981
$US ('000,000)

	1977	1978	1979	1980	1981
Antigua	-9.6	-2.2	-23.3	-39.6	-56.1
Belize	-19.2	-15.8	-29.5	-12.9	-22.0
Dominica	-5.5	-6.2	-14.1	-33.9	-21.7
Grenada	5.3	-4.4	-15.1	-15.1	-21.6
Montserrat	1.1	-0.9	-2.6	-5.9	-6.3
St. Kitts-Nevis	-1.2	-0.6	-3.2	-10.4	-11.5
St. Lucia	-11.4	-23.5	-27.9	-33.3	-51.6
St. Vincent	-6.4	0.0	-7.3	-9.4	-7.0
LDCs Total	-46.9	-53.6	-123.0	-160.5	-197.8
Barbados	-51.6	-31.5	-19.0	-5.8	-96.5
Guyana	-98.5	-28.4	-81.6	-117.6	-174.0
Jamaica	-34.6	-86.7	-142.6	-148.1	-426.8
Trinidad & Tobago	215.0	36.2	45.4	295.4	98.8
MDCs Total	30.3	-110.4	-197.8	23.9	-598.5
CARICOM Total	-16.6	-164.0	-320.8	-136.6	-796.3
(excluding Trinidad)					
MDCs Total	-184.7	-146.6	-243.2	-271.5	-697.3
CARICOM Total	-231.6	-200.2	-366.2	-432.0	-895.1

SOURCE: Marie Freckleton, "Some Thoughts on Balance of Payments Policies in the Caribbean Community," CARICOM Bulletin, no. 3 (1982), Table 1, p. 20.

end its existence. In its failure to operate successfully as a self-financing institution, the CIC was witness to the difficulty of marrying the "development" needs of the LDCs to the efficiency requirements of regional integration. The failure of the CIC to provide tangible industrial benefits to the LDCs represented a further disappointment in their hopes to share in the gains from regional integration.

The publication in 1975 of the World Bank regional study on the Caribbean provided an exhaustive analysis of the regional integration movement and gave an overall perspective on the accomplishments and future direction of CARICOM. In addition to a detailed sectoral analysis and a separate report on the Leeward and Windward Islands, the nine-volume study provided observations on the regional integration scheme. It also specifically criticized the CARICOM rules of origin and provisions for duty-free importation of inputs as well as the harmonization of fiscal incentives and instruments for industrialization, and characterized CARICOM as a "disguised free-trade area."[54] Those most closely involved with the integration movement were not unaware of these shortcomings, and the World Bank Report gave impetus to efforts to change the rules of origin, move toward a common protective policy, and reexamine the position of the LDCs.

Within the region, the overall assessment of the accomplishments and future direction of CARICOM was presented in a report prepared jointly by William Demas, who had been named president of the Caribbean Development Bank in 1974, and Alister McIntyre, who had replaced him as secretary-general of CARICOM. The report, which came to be known as the Demas-McIntyre Report, was presented at a special meeting of technicians that took place in Georgetown, Guyana, in January 1977. It began with a statement that recognized the shortcomings of the "phased freeing of trade" approach that had been adopted in Georgetown ten years earlier and evoked the need to base regional cooperation on the integration of production—an approach that was not reflected in the structure and operation of CARICOM: "One cannot repeat too often the well-known proposition that the main benefits from integration are derived not so much from the freeing of trade as from the development of complementary structures of production and demand."[55]

The report went on to advocate a "basic needs" approach to national and regional development as a means to redress the imbalance between national production and regional consumption. Integration would serve as a means whereby a large part of production of goods and services would be directed to meet the basic needs of the people— food, clothing, shelter, community health, and relevant basic education.[56] The Demas-McIntyre Report conceptually united regional integration as an example of collective self-reliance and the basic-needs approach to development, but it did not go much further in elaborating the specific ways in which that could be done within the context of CARICOM. It is significant, however, that the report reflected the conception of regional integration put forth by Havelock Brewster and Clive Y. Thomas in 1967 as well as that espoused recently by Thomas alone.[57]

The Demas-McIntyre Report identified shortcomings in the existing integration scheme and made a number of recommendations. Ten major problems were identified and discussed: (1) the licensing and restriction of intraregional trade, (2) regional import programming, (3) the arrangements for production and trade in agricultural products,

(4) state trading and public-sector procurement, (5) the financing of intraregional trade, (6) industrial complementarity through regional industrial programming, (7) instruments for external policy coordination, (8) bilateral agreements with third countries, (9) issues affecting the LDCs, and (10) machinery for monitoring and surveillance.[58]

In discussing the distributive element of CARICOM, the report pointed out that CARICOM trade is increasingly coming to mean intra-MDC trade. Moreover, even though the intraregional flow of financial resources to the LDCs as a group from the various regional institutions has been five times more (on a per capita basis) than the flow to the MDCs, there are still major constraints on LDC development. These constraints include a shortage of skilled manpower and a lack of organization, inefficient mobilization and deployment of resources, small markets, absence of a financial infrastructure, and high wage costs. Identification of these problems constitutes recognition of the fact that the *laissez-faire* approach to distributive measures is not likely to solve the problem of polarization, and that a more "positive" approach is needed to overcome the problem. Regional industrial programming is specifically mentioned as an effective redistributive tool.[59]

Industrial planning on a regional level is seen as one of the important aspects of regional integration that has not been undertaken. Necessary elements would include a common external trade policy, a common policy on foreign investment and the transfer of technology, a coordinated regional program for technological development and adaptation, and the harmonization of commercial legislation.[60] The Demas-McIntyre Report recommended, *inter alia,* the introduction of the Regime for Regional Industrial Programming, which, if adopted, would put CARICOM among the most advanced of Third World regional integration schemes. The rejection of the Draft Agreement on Foreign Investment and Development of Technology represented the rejection of this type of integration scheme, however, and the conflict over intraregional trade beginning in 1977 and continuing into 1978 did not provide a propitious atmosphere for the negotiation of measures that would transform CARICOM in this way.

Since the mid-1970s, much of the effort expended toward the advancement of CARICOM has consisted of consolidation of the existing arrangements, including adoption of the new rules of origin ratified by all twelve member countries by 1980. A new organization, the Organisation of East Caribbean States (OECS), was created on July 4, 1981, to replace the West Indies Associated States. It incorporates the East Caribbean Common Market (ECCM) countries of Antigua, Dominica, Grenada, Montserrat, St. Kitts/Nevis, St. Lucia, and St.

Vincent and has its headquarters in St. Lucia, with the Economic Secretariat remaining in Antigua. On October 1, 1983, the East Caribbean Currency Authority (ECCA) was legally converted into a central bank—namely, the East Caribbean Central Bank (ECCB). No further major steps toward deepening integration have been contemplated in a situation in which relations among governments of the region were strained by unfavorable economic conditions and deteriorating political relations in the region.[61]

In 1977, both Guyana and Jamaica placed restrictions on imports, including those from CARICOM countries. Later in the year, Trinidad and Tobago, whose petroleum exports provided a large balance-of-payments surplus, both intra- and extraregionally, threatened to retaliate in kind. This disruption of intraregional trade, which constitutes the major expansive benefit of Caribbean integration to date, has served to erode the basis for further regional cooperation, with respect to both the consolidation of the existing integration scheme and the efforts made by the CARICOM Secretariat to create a more advanced integration scheme through negotiations for further integrative measures.

In 1981, a report was completed on the state of Caribbean integration by a group of eminent persons known as the "wise men." The report analyzed the major shortcomings of CARICOM and suggested ways to advance regional integration beyond its static state. Currently, political events at the national level are distracting member states from the regional effort, and in some cases they are creating obstacles to regional cooperation.

The gaining of political independence by nearly all the Eastern Caribbean territories and Belize in the early 1980s and the unsettled political climate surrounding these events have undermined the basis for regional cooperation. In addition, the changing of regime in several territories has the potential of directly influencing regional politics. The ousting of Prime Minister Eric Gairy of Grenada by the Peoples' Revolutionary Government in 1979 led to strained relations with other governments of the region, particularly Barbados and the republic of Trinidad and Tobago. Events led to further disruption in Grenada with the assassination of Prime Minister Maurice Bishop and the subsequent invasion by the United States in 1983 to eliminate Cuban influence. By the end of 1984, elections had been held and a new government under Herbert Blaize was in power. In Jamaica, the defeat of Michael Manley's government by the Jamaica Labour party (JLP) at the end of 1980 brought to power a party that had traditionally been suspicious of regional integration and that retained power in the 1983 elections.

Given the political ferment in various countries in the region, and with the major economic sectors of sugar, bauxite, and petroleum still in decline in the earlier 1980s, it is not surprising that CARICOM has not made significant advances toward a more advanced type of integration since 1975. Within the present state of integration, however, CARICOM has succeeded in moving forward in several areas—most notably the agricultural sector. Faced with a food import crisis of major proportions, regional policy has evolved in a way that reflects the tendency of integration to respond more directly to the basic needs of the region. Thus, within the agricultural sector, CARICOM has begun to move toward regional policies that it had failed to adopt as part of the overall integration movement—namely, the restructuring of its ties of dependency on metropolitan countries, which entails a process of collective self-reliance. Full appreciation of the deep roots of Caribbean agricultural underdevelopment and dependence requires some knowledge of the historical background of agriculture in the region. The following chapter provides this background to regional agricultural policy.

Notes

1. This chapter is a revised version of an earlier article by the author entitled "Integration and Development in the Commonwealth Caribbean: The Politics of Regional Negotiations," *International Organization* 32 (Autumn 1978):953–973.

2. At the time of federation (1958–1962), a customs union was proposed as part of the federation in the Croft Report of the Trade and Tariff Commission. For comments on that proposal, see T. Balogh, "Making a Customs Union," *Social and Economic Studies* 9 (March 1960):37–40; William G. Demas, "The Economics of West Indies Customs Union," ibid., pp. 13–28; and Gerald M. Meier, "The Effects of Customs Union on Economic Development," ibid., pp. 29–36. A summary of the events leading up to the establishment of CARIFTA can be found in CARIFTA Secretariat, *CARIFTA and the New Caribbean* (Georgetown, Guyana: CARIFTA Secretariat, 1971), pp. 13–16.

3. This association is variously referred to in its own documents as the Incorporated Commonwealth Chambers of Industry and Commerce of the Caribbean, the Incorporated Chambers of Industry and Commerce of the British Caribbean, and the Incorporated Commonwealth Chambers of Commerce and Industry of the Caribbean. The organization subsequently changed its name to the Caribbean Association of Industry and Commerce (CAIC).

4. See ICCC, "Report of the Phased Freeing of Trade Delegation Which Visited Governments and Member Organizations in the Islands of Trinidad and Tobago, Grenada, Barbados, St. Vincent, St. Lucia, Dominica, Antigua, Montserrat, St. Kitts, Jamaica and Guyana, September 10th to October 9th

1966" (Port of Spain, Trinidad, October 20, 1966); Trinidad Chamber of Commerce, Inc., "A Caribbean Business Community," Discussion Paper submitted to the Directors of the ICCC (Port of Spain, Trinidad, June 10, 1965). See also the reports commissioned by the ICCC evaluation of the UWI studies and of the potential distribution of benefits in CARIFTA: E.B.A. St. Cyr, "Studies in Regional Integration: Preliminary Report" (Port of Spain, Trinidad, June 26, 1967), and E.B.A. St. Cyr, "Caribbean Economic Integration—The Distribution of Benefits with Special Reference to the Smaller Units" (Port of Spain, Trinidad, July 31, 1967).

5. See, especially, Havelock Brewster and Clive Y. Thomas, *The Dynamics of West Indian Economic Integration* (Mona, Jamaica: ISER, 1967); Steve de Castro, *The Caribbean Air Transport Industry* (Mona, Jamaica: ISER, 1967); Norman Girvan, *The Caribbean Bauxite Industry* (Mona, Jamaica: ISER, 1967).

6. Committee A of the conference dealt with the general measures of integration, Committee B dealt with the Caribbean Development Bank, and Committee C dealt with other immediately required regional institutions and services. See Conference of Commonwealth Caribbean Countries, August 14–18, 1967, *Resolution Representing Item A of the Agenda,* paras. (i)(a)–(b) and para. (iii).

7. Conference of Commonwealth Caribbean Countries, August 14–18, 1967, *Resolution on Item "B" of the Agenda.*

8. Conference of Commonwealth Caribbean Countries, *Resolution Representing Item A of the Agenda,* paras. (ii)–(viii).

9. Commonwealth Caribbean Regional Secretariat, *From CARIFTA to Caribbean Community* (Georgetown, Guyana: CARIFTA Secretariat, 1972), p. 35.

10. Economic Commission for Latin America (ECLA), Office for the Caribbean, *The Caribbean Integration Programme (1968–1972),* draft, POINT 72 8 CROP, 1 (Port of Spain, Trinidad: UN/ECLA, 1973), p. 17.

11. Caribbean Development Bank, *Annual Report 1970* (Bridgetown, Barbados: CDB, 1970).

12. Caribbean Development Bank, *Annual Report 1971* (Bridgetown, Barbados: CDB, 1971). At this time EC$1.00 was worth approximately US$.50.

13. Caribbean Development Bank, *Annual Report 1973* (Bridgetown, Barbados: CDB, 1973), p. 11.

14. William G. Demas, "Statement at the Sixteenth Session of the Economic Commission for Latin America," Port of Spain, Trinidad: UN/ECLA, May 1975, *Speeches and Resolutions,* p. 13. See also William G. Demas, "Address to the Fifth Annual Meeting of the Board of Governors," May 26 and 27, 1975 (Bridgetown, Barbados, 1975).

15. ECLA, *The Caribbean Integration Programme (1968–1972),* p. 17.

16. Economic Commission for Latin America (ECLA), Office for the Caribbean, *Economic Activity: Caribbean Community Countries—1974* (Port of Spain, Trinidad: ECLA, 1975), ECLA/POS 75/4.

17. Ibid.

18. ECLA, *The Caribbean Integration Programme (1968–1972),* p. 19.

19. A discussion and critical evaluation of the Agricultural Marketing Protocol and Guaranteed Market Scheme is provided by agricultural economist Louis L. Smith, *Critical Evaluation of the Performance of the ECCM Countries Under the Agricultural Marketing Protocol (AMP) and the Guaranteed Market Scheme (GMS),* ECLA/POS 74/6 (Port of Spain, Trinidad: ECLA, Office for the Caribbean, 1974).

20. *Advocate-News* (Barbados), 12 May 1969.

21. Ibid., 27 June 1970 and 4 October 1970.

22. *Express* (Trinidad), 6 June 1970.

23. *Daily Gleaner* (Jamaica), 25 February 1971.

24. *Express* (Trinidad), supplement, 19 July 1970.

25. *Graphic* (Guyana), 15 April 1970.

26. As early as 1969, the Barbados Manufacturers Association called for protection from third country imports. See *Advocate-News* (Barbados), 28 December 1969.

27. *Guardian* (Trinidad), 21 February 1968.

28. *Guardian* (Trinidad), 8 October 1972.

29. *Advocate-News* (Barbados), 5 October 1969.

30. *Daily Gleaner* (Jamaica), 27 April 1973.

31. *Advocate-News* (Barbados), 8 October 1971.

32. Ibid.

33. *Guardian* (Trinidad), 4 October 1971.

34. *Advocate-News* (Barbados), 18 June 1970.

35. *Guardian* (Trinidad), 11 October 1972.

36. Caribbean Association of Industry and Commerce, Inc., "Report of the Mission Undertaken by the Caribbean Association of Industry and Commerce (CAIC) to the LDCs of CARIFTA to Discuss and Stimulate the Establishment of Industrial Ventures in the LDCs," October 1972, pp. 2–3.

37. *Graphic* (Guyana), 17 October 1972.

38. *Advocate-News* (Barbados), 7 April 1973.

39. Commonwealth Caribbean Regional Secretariat, Eighth Conference of Heads of Government of Commonwealth Caribbean Countries, Georgetown, Guyana, April 9–12, 1973, *Montserrat's Proposals on the Caribbean Common Market* (submitted by Montserrat), HGC 18/73, March 30, 1973, p. 2.

40. Ibid., pp. 4–5.

41. Ibid., p. 6.

42. *Daily Gleaner* (Jamaica), 12 April 1973.

43. *Express* (Trinidad), 11 April 1973.

44. Ibid.

45. CARIFTA Secretariat, "The Georgetown Accord," *The Caribbean Community—A Guide* (Georgetown, Guyana: CARIFTA, 1973), Appendix A, pp. 93–96.

46. Caribbean Community Secretariat, *Progress in Caribbean Integration During 1973* (Georgetown, Guyana: CARICOM Secretariat, 1974), p. 13; Commonwealth Caribbean Regional Secretariat, *From CARIFTA to Caribbean*

Community, pp. 65–68. The following summary closely follows this analysis: Alister McIntyre and Beverly Watson, *Studies in Foreign Investment in the Commonwealth Caribbean: Trinidad and Tobago,* no. 1 (Mona, Jamaica: ISER, 1970). See also Beverly Watson, *Supplementary Notes on Foreign Investment in the Commonwealth Caribbean* (Mona, Jamaica: ISER, 1974); Paul L. Chen-Young, *Report on Private Investment in the Caribbean* (Kingston, Jamaica: Atlas Publishing Company, 1973).

47. Caribbean Community Secretariat, *One Year of CARICOM* (George-town, Guyana: CARICOM Secretariat, 1974), p. 33.

48. The politics of the failure of CARICOM to move up to this stage is discussed in comparison with the Andean Group's success in this area in W. Andrew Axline and Lynn K. Mytelka's "Société multinationale et intégration régionale dans le Groupe andin et dans la Communauté des Caraïbes," *Etudes internationales* 7 (June 1976):163–192.

49. See Caribbean Development Bank, *Annual Reports* (1980, 1981, 1982, and 1983) (Barbados).

50. See Caribbean Development Bank, *Annual Reports* (1983 and 1984) (Barbados).

51. CARICOM Secretariat, "Patterns of Intra-Regional Trade in the Caribbean Community, 1973–1983," *CARICOM Bulletin,* no. 5 (1984):10–44.

52. Caribbean Development Bank, *Annual Report 1977* (Barbados), pp. 48–50.

53. Caribbean Investment Corporation, *Annual Report and Statement of Accounts for the Year Ended 31st December 1976* (St. Lucia: CIC, 1976), pp. 10–15.

54. International Bank for Reconstruction and Development, International Development Association, *Caribbean Regional Study,* Report no. 566a (Washington, D.C.: IBRD, 1975), cited in the *Daily Chronicle* (Guyana), 7 July 1975.

55. "Towards the More Effective Functioning of the Caribbean Common Market," Report of Special Meeting of Technicians (Georgetown, Guyana, January 17–18, 1977), p. 1.

56. Ibid., p. 54.

57. Havelock Brewster and Clive Y. Thomas, *The Dynamics of West Indian Economic Integration;* Clive Y. Thomas, *Dependence and Transformation* (New York: Monthly Review Press, 1974).

58. "Towards the More Effective Functioning of the Caribbean Common Market," pp. 44–46.

59. Ibid., p. 28.

60. Ibid., p. 22. For a discussion of industrial planning in CARICOM, see Anthony Payne, "Regional Industrial Programming in CARICOM," in Anthony Payne and Paul Sutton, eds., *Dependency Under Challenge: The Political Economy of the Commonwealth Caribbean* (Manchester: University of Manchester Press, 1984), pp. 131–151.

61. A comprehensive analysis of the crisis in CARICOM can be found in Anthony Payne, "The Rise and Fall of Caribbean Regionalisation," *Journal of Common Market Studies* 19 (March 1981):255–280.

4
Caribbean Agricultural Development: The Challenge

If CARICOM, like other regional integration schemes among developing countries, relegated agricultural development to a subordinate position among regional priorities, it was not because this sector was free of problems. On the contrary, agriculture in the region faces major and increasing problems of low output, low productivity, and trade deficits, all of which have reached crisis proportions. The gravity of the situation is reflected in the fact that CARICOM has now begun action on a regional level that goes beyond what other integration schemes have undertaken in the agricultural sector. Regional agricultural policy in CARICOM is a response to conditions that can be traced to deep-rooted structural and institutional problems in Caribbean agriculture.

An understanding of agriculture in the West Indies is the key to understanding all other elements of Caribbean society; specifically because agriculture has played a central role in the economic, social, and political evolution of the region. In turn, an understanding of Caribbean agriculture requires knowledge of the historical context of British colonialism, slavery, and sugar. A remarkable witness to this fact is the 1975 report of the World Bank on the agricultural sector of the Commonwealth Caribbean countries, in which nearly all of the structural problems discussed reflect the legacy of historical experience from the sixteenth through the nineteenth centuries.[1]

The Nature of Plantation Society

The contemporary economic and social structure of the countries of the region can be traced directly to British colonial policy and development of sugar cultivation based on slave labor in the West Indies.[2] The literature dealing with this "plantation society" extensively analyzes the impact of the historical experience.[3] The plantation

45

economy contributed to growth in total output of the region, but it failed to lead to development. The establishment of the plantations opened up previously uncultivated lands, resulting in the creation of social and overhead capital; moreover, expanded production and income earned foreign exchange for imports of capital and consumer goods, contributed to the technology of the region, and further stimulated output through the demonstration and multiplier effects. These were net effects, for the most part, as in most instances plantation production did not displace previously existing production.

The structure of the plantation economy, however, limited the possible contribution of agriculture to development, owing mainly to the foreign ownership of the plantations, the high import content of plantation investment, and the relatively high consumer import propensity. These limits to development were further accentuated by the contribution of plantations to population growth in many of the countries. The linkages created by the plantations were tied into the structure of metropolitan plantation enterprises in the British Isles, thus generating wealth in the British economy rather than in that of the West Indies. In addition, the low skill content of plantation work contributed little to the diffusion of skills throughout the economy, leaving the plantation society marked by a highly skewed income distribution. In short, the plantation economy constituted a major impediment to development.[4]

The contemporary sociocultural structure of the West Indies is also directly rooted in the plantation economy. Plantations used compulsion and coercion in the form of slavery and indentureship to secure adequate labor supplies, and in the acquisition of this labor the racial inferiority of nonwhites became the moral justification of slavery and indentureship. The composition of the present-day population of the Caribbean countries provides a rough reflection of the same proportion of racial groups that existed on individual plantations. Accordingly, the region is now populated by descendants of a coercively transplanted people whose social structure has been defined by the requirements of the plantation economy.

In addition, the centralized control of the plantation economy has created in the countries of the Caribbean a deep-seated psychological dependence on the outside world in general and the mother country in particular—a dependence that continues as an important influence today. This psychological dependence of a hierarchical social structure based upon race has not been changed by the advent of "flag" independence for many of the countries of the region, and it continues to play an important role in the social life of the contemporary Caribbean region.

The present state of underdevelopment of the Caribbean economies is closely related to the dependence manifested in the plantation society. This dependence is reflected not only in trade patterns but also in the high degree of foreign control of the Caribbean economies in the resource and tourist sectors as well as that of plantation agriculture. The export of petroleum, bauxite, and traditional agricultural products over recent decades, while providing increases in income, has not contributed greatly to employment; moreover, it has been associated with the decline in the domestic agricultural sector and with the increase in dependence on imported foodstuffs to feed the local population. The large proportion of foreign ownership and control in the basic sectors of the economy has minimized the linkages among sectors of the economy and has resulted in insufficient use of domestic resources, national savings, and local technology. The manufacturing sector, which has shown growth over the past few decades (particularly in Jamaica and the republic of Trinidad and Tobago), has also depended heavily on direct foreign investment, often through the establishment of subsidiaries of transnational enterprises. Similarly, the tourist sector in Jamaica, Barbados, and the Eastern Caribbean has been exploited by foreign enterprise, with the result that linkages to the rest of the economy have become limited.[5] Most striking has been the failure of the increased tourist activity to establish greater links between tourism and agriculture; indeed, in the agricultural sector, food imports have been even further inflated in the interests of catering to metropolitan tastes.

The far-reaching effects on present-day economic, social, and political life in the Caribbean deriving from the plantation system stem from the type of agricultural production imposed on the West Indies by England in order to cultivate and export sugar to the homeland.[6] The historical background of sugar production, subsistence agriculture, and agricultural policies pursued by the colonial government and, more recently, by national governments of the region provides a basis for understanding the politics of agriculture in the region today.

The Colonial Legacy

The Portuguese, who originally developed the plantation system in the New World, introduced the cultivation of sugar cane in North East Brazil; their use of African slaves was an idea borrowed from the Muslims. The first Europeans in the Caribbean were Spaniards, beginning with the expeditions of Columbus for the Spanish crown in search of precious metals. They were followed by the Dutch, French, and English, who found three kinds of Caribbean locations: the densely forested Guyana coast, the densely forested Caribbean coast of Central America, and the smaller islands of the Antilles. These last were especially advantageous for colonization because they were less distant from European ports; they were small; and each one had its own dock, thereby reducing the amount of overland transportation and making it very difficult for slaves to escape.[7]

Integration of the West Indies into the economy of Europe took place early, under the mercantilist system of trade in raw materials specifically selected to aid the growth of the metropole in exchange for certain industrial goods at steadily controlled and inflated prices.[8] Thus, with the consolidation of the British West Indies, the Caribbean region became the tropical farms of the British nation. This system of exploitation was based both on a social structure rooted in slavery and on the importation of slaves to the Western hemisphere, estimated to number over 15 million in the period from 1501 to 1865.[9]

The key element of slavery was racism. This ideology saw the Amerindians as an inferior form of animal life and, thus, as subordinate by nature to the European colonists. In addition, the Christian faith was held out as the only way to gain the status of (subordinate) humanity. In the case of Africans, racism was used more broadly to legitimize outright exploitation and was extended systematically to cultural, physical, genetic, and biological attributes of nonwhite people.[10] By defining inferiority in terms of physical and cultural attributes, the Europeans guaranteed that no matter how "Europeanized" Africans might become, they remained Negroes and thus, by definition, slaves.[11] Race, then, became the basis of the class structure, which played an essential role in the economic development of the West Indies in the nineteenth and twentieth centuries. The contemporary economic structure of Caribbean societies, particularly the agricultural sector, can be traced to the relationship between people and the land defined by slavery and the plantation economy.

The history of development of the West Indian peasantry is circumscribed by the existence of the plantation system, with present-day conditions still reflecting the peasants' struggle to break through an institutional setting biased toward agricultural stagnation.[12] Given the circumstances of their origins, the West Indian agricultural workers do not fit the conventional definition of the peasant. They have no history of long ties of tradition and sentiment to the land they control, nor are they the expression of a rural dimension of an old civilization.[13] The peasantry, which originated at the time of emancipation in 1838, is composed of ex-slaves who started farms on the peripheries of plantations and who exist alongside and in conflict with the plantation.[14]

The first settlers in the Leeward Islands were smallholders who cultivated tobacco, cotton, and indigo with the aid of a few white laborers. This experience ended with the advent of sugar, which brought slavery. The smallholders led a precarious existence facing heavy import duties, and the land passed into the hands of magnates who rapidly amassed large fortunes, thus marking the beginnings of plantation agriculture.[15] Cultivation of sugar was so profitable that no rival crop was introduced, rotation was not practiced, and alternative types of husbandry were not undertaken. British colonial policy strove for the creation and maintenance of a strong, self-sufficient Empire, and legislation was adopted to achieve this end. Three acts—the Navigation Act of 1660, the Staple Act of 1663, and the Plantation Act of 1673—gave the West Indian colonies a virtual monopoly over the expanding sugar market and guaranteed a valuable market for tools, clothing, and provisions produced in England.[16]

The Windward Islands of Grenada, St. Vincent, and Dominica were added to the Empire by the Treaty of Paris in 1763, and St. Lucia was added in 1803. In the newly acquired Windwards, the cultivation of sugar was established through the squeezing out of smallholders, but these islands were only partially exploited at the time of the abolition of slave trade in 1807 and thus were only half as thickly populated with slaves as the Leewards had been at the time of final registration in 1832.

The Act of Emancipation in 1838 gave civil status to slaves, thus enabling them to acquire land. In Jamaica, Guyana, the Windwards, and to some extent in Trinidad and Tobago there was some opportunity to acquire land, but in the Leewards and Barbados there was scarcely any land to be had. Little attempt was made by the British government to encourage the development of small farms, and the large planters sought from the beginning to obstruct peasant land settlement.[17] The beginnings of the West Indian peasantry occurred with the movement of slaves away from the plantation to start farms on the peripheral lands—an event that created the classic conflict between peasant and plantation production that stands at the root of many of the contemporary problems of rural development in the region.

Peasant land settlement would confirm the worst fears of the planters and disrupt their economy. Accordingly, they sought from the beginning to obstruct peasant land settlement through a number of measures: labor rent tenancy and long labor contracts, a system of license fees for employment outside the estates, and licenses and fees that made it difficult for the ex-slaves to produce staple crops or to employ themselves in the production of charcoal, firewood, or arrowroot flour. Above all else, they blocked extensive peasant settlement on uncul-

tivated land.[18] As previously noted, land in Barbados and the Leeward Islands was particularly scarce. In Guyana and Trinidad, planters replaced slaves who had left the plantations with thousands of indentured workers brought in mainly from India. In the Windwards, the peasantry was better able to establish itself, as the plantation system never gained dominance to the degree it had in other territories and peasants had greater access to the land. As a result, these islands today more closely resemble peasant communities than do any of the other islands in the West Indies.[19]

In the century and a half since emancipation, the peasantry in the region has still not managed to secure much of the agricultural land and other resources, and the situation has largely reverted to the pattern that existed just after emancipation.[20] In addition to the restrictions on the advancement of the peasantry imposed by the control of the plantations over basic agricultural resources, the potential of peasant development was never fully realized because government policy has tended to ignore the existence of the class. This neglect can be explained by the dominance of the estate-based sugar industry over influential opinion, both in the region and in the metropole. Planters feared that peasant expansion would ruin the sugar industry by creating labor shortages, whereas metropolitan officials believed that the continued prosperity and civilization of the West Indies were dependent on the survival of the estate-based industry. The attitude of the government was modified only in times of crisis caused by discontent and restlessness among laborers and depression in the sugar industry.[21]

The report of the West Indies Royal Commission of 1897 seemed to point in a new direction. It reflected the recognition that the peasantry was a source of political and economic strength, and thus recommended land settlement and diversification of agriculture. C. Y. Shephard describes the report as "the Magna Carta of the West Indian peasant."[22] In Jamaica, a land settlement scheme had been started in 1896, but before 1897 government policy had done nothing to encourage peasant farming in the Leewards and Windwards.[23] In 1899 the government of St. Vincent initiated an extensive land settlement scheme, as did Carriacou in 1903. Antigua was the first of the Leeward Islands to establish such a policy in 1916. Similar schemes were eventually started in Dominica, Nevis, and Anguilla, and were then extended to other islands in the 1930s.[24] These schemes were generally disappointing, with settlement occurring mainly on land on which estate enterprise had failed or on land that had been too poor to be used, and with little attention being paid to the choice of settlers for the land or to problems of the small farmers' deficiencies

in knowledge, capital, and organization.[25] The schemes were pursued not as consistent and coherent policy but, rather, as expedients when crisis threatened in the 1920s, 1930s, and 1940s.

The Sugar Commission of 1929-1930 drew attention to the regrettable fact that not much had been done to implement the 1897 recommendations, and it called for further attempts at land settlement and agricultural diversification. These sentiments had to be repeated in the report of the Moyne Commission in 1939.[26] It was not until the 1940s, after widespread disturbances, that any sustained attempt was made to implement the recommendations.[27]

In Trinidad and Guyana, where large numbers of indentured laborers had been brought in to work on plantations, their settlement on the land was viewed as a means to avoid repatriation costs. Some 32,000 acres were provided for Indians in Guyana from 1891 to 1913, 23,000 acres in Trinidad from 1885 to 1895, and another 31,766 acres in Trinidad and Tobago from 1902 to 1912.[28]

The history of land settlement schemes in the Caribbean has been characterized as dismal.[29] Some of the reasons for their failure were as follows: (1) the small size of holdings resulting from the need to reach the largest number of farmers; (2) the lack of capital and low level of technology; (3) the absence of "managerial" thinking; and (4) inappropriate locations, which resulted in farms that were not economically viable.[30] It is not surprising that the traditional export sector continued to dominate agriculture in the region and that the structure of agriculture has remained basically unchanged. In the Commonwealth Caribbean today, 95 percent of the 350,000 farm holdings are under 25 acres in size, and these amount to less than 30 percent of the total acreage of farms.[31]

Caribbean Agriculture: Problems and Obstacles

During World War II, when shipping lanes were blocked, the region was able to go a long way toward feeding itself through efforts focused on satisfying local basic needs. Since then, approximately 500,000 acres of arable land in the region have either gone out of production or been underutilized.[32] As a result of the large influx of capital into the region to develop the extractive sector (petroleum in Trinidad and bauxite in Guyana and Jamaica), to pursue policies of industrialization by invitation in the 1950s and 1960s, and to promote tourism, domestic food production was relegated to last place relative to these activities and export agriculture. In Trinidad, indications are that development of the petroleum industry has had little direct adverse effect on the use of agricultural land.[33] Similarly, bauxite in

Guyana and bauxite and tourism in Jamaica have not been major competitors for land,[34] although in some Eastern Caribbean territories such as Montserrat, the tourist industry has resulted in significant losses of arable land.[35] All of these industries have had a more direct effect on agricultural labor. Higher wages in the extractive, industrial, and tourist sectors have increased the reserve price of agricultural labor, but without accompanying rises in agricultural productivity. Relatively low agricultural wages combined with the traditional disdain for agricultural work have produced high levels of unemployment side by side with labor shortages in the agricultural sector.[36]

As a result of the low wages in agriculture and the widening gap between agricultural and industrial incomes, a population drift from rural to urban areas has occurred. Comparative data on wages in the agricultural sector and the general economy are provided in Table 4.1. In the period from 1960 to 1970, the Caribbean region witnessed a reduction by one-third of agricultural employment and a 25 percent drop in land under cultivation.[37] Data on land use in the region are provided in Table 4.2. In Montserrat from 1957 to 1972, farming land fell from 17,240 acres to 5,860 acres, and from 1954 to 1976 the total number of farms fell by 60 percent. In Trinidad and Tobago, 10 percent to 15 percent of farmland is no longer cultivated. In Jamaica, total land in farms went from 1,822,800 acres in 1958 to 1,489,000 in 1968, whereas 83,000 acres in farms over 100 acres in size were idle (70 percent of this latter territory constituted land of the highest quality). In Barbados, 15,000 acres, representing 20 percent of the arable land, are now idle or underutilized. Throughout the region, approximately half a million acres of cultivable land is idle or underutilized.[38] The productivity of the land is further limited by the fragmentation that has resulted from the division of holdings by inheritance and "parcelization" (i.e., the geographical dispersion of a single farmer's land).[39]

It has been estimated that 32 percent of the population of the region is supported by agriculture—a figure that dropped from 47.1 percent in 1953 to 33.7 percent in 1973 in Jamaica, dropped from 37.1 percent in 1960 to 20.5 percent in 1972 in Guyana, and remained stable at about 20.5 percent in Trinidad.[40] Of the region's 350,000 farm holdings, 95 percent are of fewer than 25 acres in size and constitute less than 30 percent of the total acreage occupied by farms. Holdings of more than 100 acres account for more than 50 percent of the total acreage but for only 2 percent of the holdings in the MDCs and less than 7 percent in the LDCs.[41] This situation, in which a small number of large estates hold a large proportion of cultivated land while a large number of small farms occupy a small share of

Table 4.1

CARICOM Countries:
Comparative Weekly Wages in Agriculture
and in the General Economy, 1973
($EC)

	Agricultural Worker	General Worker
Barbados	27/36	42/48
Guyana	30	32
Jamaica	29/42	25/83
Trinidad & Tobago	15/25	24/45
Antigua	36	40
Dominica	15/20	24/30
Grenada	15/25	15/25
Montserrat	n.a	35
St. Kitts	40	20/25
St. Lucia	21	16/20
St. Vincent	15/20	15/20
Belize	23	20/28

SOURCE: International Bank for Reconstruction and Development, International Development Agency, Caribbean Regional Study (Washington, D.C.: IBRD, 1975).

the land, results in a negligible amount of full-time family farming on medium-sized farms (25–100 acres). Data on the area and number of land holdings are provided in Tables 4.3 and 4.4.

Moreover, the low level of technical knowledge among small farmers due to inadequacy of extension services has resulted in low agricultural output and high production costs. Infrastructure limitations, such as inadequate feeder roads and a poorly organized marketing system, have also impeded the development of the local food sector, with governments placing emphasis on the development of export agriculture

Table 4.2

CARICOM Countries:
Land Use as a Percent of Total Land Area, 1979

	Arable Land	Permanent Crops	Meadows and Pastures	Total Area Agriculture	Forest Land	Other	Total Land Area
LDCs							
Antigua	----18.2----		6.8	25.0	15.9	59.1	100
Belize	3.4	0.5	1.6	5.5	44.4	50.1	100
Dominica	9.3	13.3	2.7	25.3	41.3	33.3	100
Grenada	5.9	35.3	5.9	47.1	11.8	41.1	100
Montserrat	----10.0----		10.0	20.0	40.0	40.0	100
St. Kitts-Nevis	22.2	16.7	2.8	41.7	16.7	41.7	100
St. Lucia	8.2	19.7	4.9	32.8	18.0	49.2	100
St. Vincent	38.2	11.8	5.9	55.9	41.2	2.9	100
MDCs							
Barbados	----76.7----		9.3	86.0	0.0	14.0	100
Guyana	1.8	0.1	5.1	7.0	92.4	0.6	100
Jamaica	18.9	5.5	19.4	43.8	28.3	27.9	100
Trinidad & Tobago	13.6	17.2	2.1	32.9	45.0	22.0	100

SOURCE: United Nations/Economic Commission for Latin America, Office for the Caribbean, _Agricultural Statistics Caribbean Countries, 1982_, CEPAL/CARIB82/13, (Port of Spain, Trinidad: UN/ECLA, 1982), Table 10.

Table 4.3

CARICOM Countries:
Area of Agricultural Holdings by Size Groups
(Hectares)

	Year	Size Groups (Hectares)								
		0-0.4	0.4-2	2-4	4-10	10-20	20+	2'40	40+	Total
LDCs										
Antigua	1961	----3,885----		n.a.	n.a.	n.a.	n.a.	1,942	8,176	14,003
Belize	n.a.	n.a.	n.a.	n.a.	n.a.	n.a.	n.a.	n.a.	n.a.	n.a.
Dominica	1961	354	3,715	----8,217----			18,549	0	0	30,835
Grenada	1975	1,016	4,255	1,987	1,915	1,055	8,669	0	0	18,897
Montserrat	1975	88	382	177	173	75	1,477	0	0	2,372
St. Kitts-Nevis	1975	281	1,139	----570----		----14,776----		0	0	16,766
St. Lucia	1973/74	702	3,430	2,862	2,589	2,550	17,018	0	0	29,151
St. Vincent	1972	533	2,738	1,645	834	418	7,740	0	0	13,908
MDCs										
Barbados	1961	----4,573----		n.a.	n.a.	n.a.	n.a.	1,700	27,924	34,197
Guyana	n.a.	n.a.	n.a.	n.a.	n.a.	n.a.	n.a.	n.a.	n.a.	n.a.
Jamaica	1968/69	----92,764----		n.a.	n.a.	n.a.	n.a.	189,385	320,525	602,674
Trinidad & Tobago	1957/58	----23,837----		n.a.	n.a.	n.a.	n.a.	76,448	90,167	190,452

SOURCE: United Nations/Economic Commission for Latin America, Office for the Caribbean, *Agricultural Statistics Caribbean Countries, 1982*, CEPAL/CARIB82/13, (Port of Spain, Trinidad: UN/ECLA, 1982), Table 5.

Table 4.4

CARICOM Countries: Number of Agricultural Holdings by Size Group

		Size of Groups (Hectares)								
	Year	Landless	0-0.4	0.5-2	2-4	4-10	10.1-20	20+	2-40	40+	Total
LDCs											
Antigua	1961	n.a.	5,233		n.a.	n.a.	n.a.	n.a.	476	38	5,747
Belize	n.a.	n.a.	n.a.		n.a.	n.a.	n.a.	n.a.	n.a.	n.a.	n.a.
Dominica	1961	n.a.	2,115	4,290	2,087			175	0	0	8,667
Grenada	1957	n.a.	12,265		n.a.	n.a.	n.a.	n.a.	1,675	99	14,039
Montserrat	1975	88	551	496	66	28	6	12	0	0	1,247
St. Kitts-Nevis	1975	n.a.	2,036	1,222	161			106	0	0	3,525
St. Lucia	1973/74	502	4,730	3,828	1,082	475	199	122	0	0	10,938
St. Vincent	1972	706	3,032	3,171	659	161	28	37	0	0	7,794
MDCs											
Barbados	1961	n.a.	18,313		n.a.	n.a.	n.a.	n.a.	292	193	18,798
Guyana	n.a.	n.a.	n.a.		n.a.	n.a.	n.a.	n.a.	n.a.	n.a.	n.a.
Jamaica	1968/69		151,705		n.a.	n.a.	n.a.	n.a.	40,662	992	193,359
Trinidad & Tobago	1957/58	n.a.	14,800		n.a.	n.a.	n.a.	n.a.	14,800	313	29,913

SOURCE: United Nations/Economic Commission for Latin America, Office for the Caribbean, Agricultural Statistics Caribbean Countries, 1982, CEPAL/CARIB82/13, (Port of Spain, Trinidad: UN/ECLA, 1982), Table 6.

and pricing policies geared to satisfy the political needs of low consumer prices.[42]

The lack of capital suffered by the food sector has resulted in the dilapidation and neglect of farms—problems that, in turn, have been aggravated by the shortage of adequate credit to small farmers and the continuing rise in cost of agricultural inputs.[43] A combination of other factors has also contributed to the decline of agriculture in the Caribbean: adverse weather conditions and natural disasters, declining soil fertility, advancing age of farmers, abandonment of land, lack of physical planning, failure of agrarian reform, inadequate technical services, and poor technology.[44]

Currently, agriculture is in decline in the Commonwealth Caribbean, although it still remains the largest source of employment in the region, accounting for about 17 percent of GDP and absorbing 22.5 percent of the working population. Data for individual countries are provided in Table 4.5. Although agricultural stagnation pervades the entire region, the impact of this trend on the overall economy varies from country to country. Agriculture plays a less important role as a source of income and employment in Trinidad and Tobago, Jamaica, and Barbados, but it is crucial to the economies of the LDCs and Guyana.[45]

In Trinidad and Tobago, the contribution of the agricultural sector to GDP declined from 4.4 percent in 1973 to 3.0 percent in 1981 in current prices, whereas the annual growth rate of the sector declined from 14.5 percent in 1978 to 4.0 percent in 1979 with the real value of output increasing by 7 percent in 1981.[46] Sugar production declined by 161,994 tons in 1979 (a fall of 3 percent from the 1978 level) and it declined to 102,045.2 tons in 1981. Agricultural production also fell in most other subsectors, two exceptions being meat and oranges, which saw significant increases.[47] Agricultural employment dropped by 4,800 jobs during 1979, principally the result of agricultural labor drifting to the construction and service sectors.[48] Because of the position of Trinidad and Tobago as a petroleum-producing economy, the impact on economic growth and foreign exchange of the decline in agriculture in this area was relatively minor compared to some of the other Caribbean countries.

In Jamaica, bauxite mining, alumina production, tourism, and manufacturing make important contributions to the national economy. In recent years, manufacturing and construction have been sluggish; although the agricultural sector has performed below its potential, it has been relatively more buoyant than most other sectors. The year 1979 saw poor performance of export crops, but this situation was counterbalanced somewhat by increases in domestic food crops, espe-

Table 4.5

CARICOM Countries:
Contribution of Agriculture to Gross Domestic Product
and Active Population in Agriculture, 1980

	Total Population	Active Population	Active in Agriculture	% Active in Agriculture	Agriculture as % of GDP
Antigua	75,000	22,000	2,000	9.1	6.4
Belize	145,000	47,000	14,000	29.8	31.4
Dominica	74,000	n.a.	n.a.	n.a.	38.2
Grenada	98,000	n.a.	n.a.	n.a.	31.9[d]
Montserrat	12,000	4,000	1,000	25.0	6.6
St. Kitts-Nevis	44,000	14,000 .	5,000	35.7	18.5[e]
St. Lucia	116,000	37,000	14,000	37.8	12.8
St. Vincent	99,000	n.a.	n.a.	n.a.	13.7
LDCs Total	663,000	124,000[e]	36,000[a]	29.0[a]	19.9
Barbados	254,000	108,000	18,000	16.7	7.7
Guyana	884,000	288,000	63,000	21.9	23.4
Jamaica	2,183,000	992	264	26.6	8.4
Trinidad & Tobago	1,067,000	n.a.	n.a.	n.a.	2.4
MDCs Total	4,388,000	396,992[b]	81,264[b]	20.5[b]	12.6
CARICOM Total	5,051,000	520,992[c]	117,264[c]	22.5[c]	16.8

SOURCE: United Nations/Economic Commission for Latin America, Office for the
Caribbean, Agricultural Statistics Caribbean Countries, 1982, CEPAL/CARIB82/13,
(Port of Spain, Trinidad: UN/ECLA, 1982), Tables 2, 4.1-4.17.

[a] Excludes Dominica, Grenada, and St. Vincent.
[b] Excludes Trinidad and Tobago.
[c] Excludes Dominica, Grenada, St. Vincent, and Trinidad and Tobago.
[d] Data for 1979.
[e] Data for 1978.

cially vegetable staples; then, in 1981, overall improvement occurred
after two years of negative growth.[49] The agricultural sector remains
crucial to the economy of Jamaica, in spite of the contributions of
tourism, mining, and manufacturing, in that it provided 36 percent
of total employment in 1979, up from 33 percent in 1975.[50] The
recent economic crisis in Jamaica, which caused a shortage of foreign
exchange, seems to have created the opportunity to stimulate agricultural employment and production.

In recent years, the economy of Barbados has been one of the
strongest in the region, showing expansion in 1980 for the fifth

consecutive year. In 1981, this trend changed with a decline in real growth of 2.6 percent. In 1979, Barbados was the only country in the region to show a significant increase in sugar production, thus contributing to a 15.9 percent increase in the agricultural sector over 1978; by 1981, however, this situation had reversed itself, with a drop of 30.3 percent from the previous year.[51] The nonexport subsector of agriculture showed no substantial growth in 1979, and indications are that performance was below 1977 levels, with declines in root crops, vegetables, and pork production, and increases in poultry and milk.[52] The contribution of agriculture to GDP based on constant 1974 prices declined from 14.6 percent in 1970 to 10.8 percent in 1979, 9.8 percent in 1980, and 7.7 percent in 1981.[53]

Guyana, though a major exporter of bauxite and alumina, is more dependent on agriculture than the other MDCs of the region—namely, Trinidad and Tobago, Jamaica, and Barbados. Rice and sugar constitute the major agricultural commodities and account for approximately 60 percent of agriculture's contribution to GDP, which in turn accounted for 22 percent of total GDP in 1981 and was the single largest sector at that time.[54] In 1979 a decline in agriculture occurred with significant drops in production of sugar, but by 1981 production was on the rise even though earnings continued to decline. The initial decline was offset somewhat by increases in the other agricultural sectors—principally rice, forestry, and fishing. However, food production was disappointing, with declines in production of root and tree crops and vegetables, in spite of a continued strategy toward increasing self-sufficiency in a wider range of foodstuffs.[55] Within the region, Guyana's resource endowment, particularly in land, makes it the territory with the greatest potential for increased agricultural production. Currently, the vast majority of this area is undeveloped hinterland.

Among the eight LDCs of the region, Belize is unique in its land resource endowment. Belize occupies 90 percent of the total territory of the CARICOM LDCs but is inhabited by only 20 percent of their population. It is also quite different in terms of resource endowment from the other seven less developed territories of the Eastern Caribbean. Agricultural production in Belize stagnated in 1978 and 1979, with declines occurring in sugar and citrus and output in the other major crops remaining stable, but production increased in 1980 and 1981.[56] Because of the large amount of potentially cultivable land in Belize, this country (along with Guyana) has the capacity to play a major role in the agricultural development of the region.

In the Eastern Caribbean LDCs, agriculture was the single largest source of employment in 1970, accounting for 32 percent of the employed population in the LDCs.[57] The sectoral composition of the labor force and the contribution of agriculture to GDP have been changing, with substantial differences being recorded among the territories. Most dramatic have been the declines in output and employment in a number of territories, particularly St. Kitts, Antigua, and Montserrat.

Production in the agricultural sector of the LDCs has been unimpressive over the past few years, with prolonged output declines occurring in all major crops. Banana output decreased in St. Vincent from 33,060 tons in 1976 to 30,856 tons in 1978, whereas Grenada's output in 1978 was 20,607 tons, roughly the same quantity as that in 1975.[58] In Dominica banana production remained stagnant between 1975 and 1977, whereas in St. Kitts-Nevis sugar production declined from 42,978 tons in 1967 to 27,550 tons in 1975, recovering to 39,672 tons in 1976.[59] In St. Lucia agriculture declined significantly in its contribution to GDP from 1970 to 1979, with production in the main crops of bananas, cocoa beans, spices, coconuts, and vegetables remaining level from 1978 to 1979. Similarly, nontraditional agriculture made no advances in 1979.[60] The most drastic change has been observed in Antigua and Montserrat, with the agricultural contribution to GDP declining from approximately 25 percent and 40 percent, respectively, to less than 5 percent in both countries by 1978. In Antigua the decline in production is largely attributable to the political decision to cease production of sugar and to the disappearance of cotton production, whereas in Montserrat it is partially attributable to the conversion of farmland into housing estates for vacation villas.[61]

In the early 1980s, the Windward Islands were concentrating on rehabilitating the agricultural sector, which had been devastated by a series of natural disasters. Among the East Caribbean territories, Antigua, St. Lucia, and Grenada had a tourist industry that made a significant contribution to GDP, but industrial production in the LDCs remained relatively insignificant, leaving agriculture as the major source of revenue and foreign exchange. Agriculture was in very poor condition in this mainly agricultural subregion.

Although there are significant differences in economic structure and agricultural production among the member countries of CARICOM, it is clear that the agricultural sector of the region is in decline. Per capita food production has dropped over the past fifteen years, resulting in an increase in the region's food trade deficit. Agricultural production for export fell by about 40 percent from the mid-1960s to the mid-1970s, reflecting a significant drop in the total amount of land under cultivation and a movement of population away from the farm. Even with agriculture's decline of importance in the regional economy, it still accounts for a significant proportion of GDP and employment.[62]

On the other hand, the region is heavily dependent on food imports, a dependency that has been growing dramatically in recent years, whereas exports of traditional agricultural crops (sugar, bananas, citrus) account for a large proportion of regional export earnings.[63] Food exports accounted for 66 percent of the export earnings of LDCs in 1976 and more than 40 percent from Barbados and Guyana in 1980. They accounted for 10.6 percent of Jamaica's export earnings and less than 2 percent of Trinidad and Tobago's. Data on food exports are provided in Table 4.6, and data on food imports are provided in Table 4.7.

As a result of the trends just described, the region has exhibited a large and growing deficit in foodstuffs that totaled US$450 million in 1978, or about US$80 per capita. In 1980, the region had become a net importer of food with agricultural products valued at US$800 million.[64] The major food items composing these imports are animal proteins—meat, dairy, and fish products, and animal feed—which make up more than 50 percent of the total value of food imports. Fruits and vegetables make up 9 percent, and oils and fats account for 4 percent.[65]

In 1978 it was estimated that 44 percent of the population of the region did not receive the minimum recommended levels of protein requirements and that 56 percent did not receive the minimum recommended levels of calorie requirements.[66] In the face of this food crisis, member governments have initiated a variety of policies designed to increase self-sufficiency, diversify agricultural production, and reduce the agricultural trade deficit. Jamaica has pursued a number of policies aimed at stimulating agricultural production, including Operation GROW (Growing and Reaping our Wealth) in 1972.[67] The republic of Trinidad and Tobago has created the Food and Agricultural Corporation, a state organization designed to participate directly in agricultural production as part of an overall food strategy.[68] Guyana has banned imports of foodstuffs for which substitutes can be grown locally, and experiments in farm cooperatives have been launched in Guyana, Jamaica, Montserrat, and Grenada. The Eastern Caribbean territories have been much more limited in their capability to mount agricultural programs because of their lack of research and administrative resources, and virtually no agricultural planning on a national level has occurred in this subregion.

National policies have not been able to prevent a growing food import bill and an increasing regional agricultural deficit—problems that reached crisis proportions in the early 1980s. But their ineffec-

Table 4.6

CARICOM Countries:
Food Exports as a Proportion of Total Exports, 1972-1980
(Percent of Total)

	1972	1973	1974	1975	1976	1977	1978	1979	1980
Antigua	1.3	0.5	0.3	0.6	12.0	7.7	5.3	n.a.	n.a.
Belize	79.1	74.9	79.1	89.8	68.0	74.0	78.2	n.a.	n.a.
Dominica	81.7	84.5	87.3	88.4	80.7	78.6	75.8	63.5	41.4
Grenada	98.5	98.6	97.5	97.2	98.5	n.a.	n.a.	n.a.	92.2
Montserrat	47.5	65.2	80.1	69.4	58.0	23.4	14.5	42.8	11.5
St. Kitts-Nevis	66.5	47.0	59.2	63.9	62.6	70.0	77.2	72.8	n.a.
St. Lucia	65.2	72.1	73.0	60.5	53.2	53.8	57.7	57.5	38.9
St. Vincent	82.5	85.5	92.5	91.6	94.7	93.6	93.4	85.7	n.a.
LDCs Mean	65.3	66.0	71.1	70.2	66.0	57.3[a]	57.4[a]	64.5[b]	46.0[c]
Barbados	63.7	57.2	61.6	58.2	57.4	48.4	38.9	55.1	41.2
Guyana	49.0	42.1	60.0	61.3	50.8	42.0	48.1	46.2	43.0
Jamaica	21.3	20.8	16.8	25.6	16.9	16.7	14.6	13.5	10.6
Trinidad & Tobago	8.4	6.2	3.9	5.9	3.4	3.0	2.7	2.7	1.8
MDCs Mean	35.6	31.6	35.6	37.8	32.1	27.5	26.1	29.4	24.2
CARICOM Mean	55.4	54.6	59.3	59.4	54.7	46.5[a]	46.0[a]	48.9[b]	35.1[c]

SOURCE: United Nations/Economic Commission for Latin America, Office for the Caribbean, Agricultural Statistics Caribbean Countries, 1982, CEPAL/CARIB82/13, (Port-of-Spain, Trinidad: UN/ECLA, 1982), Table 50.

[a] Excludes Grenada.
[b] Excludes Antigua, Belize, and Dominica.
[c] Excludes Antigua, Belize, St. Kitts-Nevis, and St. Vincent.

Table 4.7

CARICOM Countries:
Food Imports as a Proportion of Total Imports, 1972-1980
(Percent of Total)

	1972	1973	1974	1975	1976	1977	1978	1979	1980
Antigua	18.1	15.8	15.2	16.9	22.8	25.8	28.8	41.9	34.3
Belize	24.8	26.0	25.8	28.3	24.1	22.3	24.3	24.0	23.2
Dominica	25.9	32.4	32.1	31.6	33.3	28.4	29.0	25.0	20.0
Grenada	31.1	34.1	40.7	34.8	32.4	n.a.	n.a.	n.a.	28.9
Montserrat	21.5	23.8	24.4	27.3	25.0	27.5	23.0	21.0	20.9
St. Kitts-Nevis	24.5	23.0	27.7	20.8	23.1	23.0	24.5	21.0	n.a.
St. Lucia	19.2	23.3	24.5	25.1	24.0	20.2	20.6	19.1	18.6
St. Vincent	29.0	30.2	29.6	32.3	31.9	28.1	32.7	33.7	n.a.
LDCs Mean	24.3	26.1	27.5	27.1	27.1	25.0[a]	26.1[a]	26.5[a]	24.3[b]
Barbados	24.2	24.0	24.8	23.3	22.1	20.6	22.1	17.6	17.6
Guyana	13.9	13.5	7.8	5.9	6.1	8.1	8.8	7.7	6.2
Jamaica	14.5	12.4	13.1	11.6	14.0	6.7	19.0	6.5	6.2
Trinidad & Tobago	9.1	10.3	6.6	8.8	6.5	8.4	9.3	10.6	9.3
MDCs Mean	15.4	15.1	13.1	12.4	12.2	11.0	14.8	10.6	9.8
CARICOM Mean	21.3	22.4	22.7	22.2	22.1	19.9[a]	22.0[a]	20.7[a]	18.5[b]

SOURCE: United Nations/Economic Commission for Latin America, Office for the Caribbean, Agricultural Statistics Caribbean Countries, 1982, CEPAL/CARIB82/13, (Port of Spain, Trinidad: UN/ECLA, 1982), Table 48.

a Excludes Grenada.
b Excludes St. Kitts-Nevis and St. Vincent.

tiveness is not surprising given the magnitude and multitude of obstacles facing food production in the region, as well as the inadequacy of the response to these problems on the part of the governments of the region.

The catalogue of these current obstacles reflects the historical development of the problems involved in transforming the agricultural sector. The land tenure system of small, intensively cultivated, fragmented holdings on poorer lands and underutilization of richer land in large plantations is at the base of the problem. In addition, infrastructure—including feeder roads, transport, marketing, and storage facilities—is inadequate, particularly in the food subsector, which does not benefit from the commodity associations that have been organized for traditional export crops. Small farmers, who make up the majority of producers of local agriculture, operate with a relatively low level of technical and managerial skills and with very little capital input. National efforts at providing extension services to help overcome these problems have been grossly inadequate. Agricultural research in the region has been almost exclusively devoted to traditional export crops, and agricultural education is limited to a few secondary schools in the region. Agricultural wages are low, particularly in comparison to the tourist, extractive, and industrial sectors—a situation that further aggravates the employment problem in the agricultural sector. Moreover, agricultural credit is inadequate and difficult for the small farmer to obtain.

Years of dependence on food imports from metropolitan countries have led to acquired tastes for these foods and limited the possibility of import substitution. This problem is further exacerbated by the high import content of food used in the tourist sector of the region. The limited scope of intraregional imports of foodstuffs (at most 15 percent of the regional food bill)[69] has not helped to offset this problem. Governments of the region that have initiated policies of agricultural diversification and import substitution have often pursued rationalization of the sector on a national scale while ignoring the regional context.

When these problems are considered in conjunction with the fact that CARICOM is composed of twelve noncontiguous territories forming an archipelago that is very limited in arable land area (given the mountainous topography of the region) and featuring a tropical ecology subject to natural disasters on a major scale, the challenge of Caribbean agricultural development appears very great indeed.

In the face of this challenge, steps have been taken at the regional level. Within CARICOM, policies have been formulated on a broad front to attack the roots of the agricultural problems. These efforts constitute a new impetus in Caribbean integration—an impetus that reflects a new insight into the broader process of integration among developing countries.

Notes

1. International Bank for Reconstruction and Development/International Development Association (IBRD/IDA), *Caribbean Regional Study,* Report no. 566A, vol. 3: Agriculture (Washington, D.C.: IBRD, 1975).

2. Eric Williams, *Capitalism and Slavery* (London: Andre Deutsch, 1964).

3. Lloyd Best and Kari Levitt, *Externally Propelled Growth and Industrialization* (Montreal: McGill University, Centre for Developing Area Studies, 1969); Lloyd Best, "A Model of Pure Plantation Economy," *Social and Economic Studies* 17 (1968); George Beckford, *Persistent Poverty: Underdevelopment in Plantation Economies of the Third World* (New York: Oxford University Press, 1972). The present analysis of the "plantation economy" relies heavily on Beckford.

4. Beckford, *Persistent Poverty,* p. 210.

5. Havelock Brewster, "Economic Dependence: A Quantitative Interpretation," *Social and Economic Studies* 22 (March 1973):90–95.

6. A penetrating analysis of the impact of plantation society on the contemporary situation in Jamaica is found in George Beckford and Michael Witter, *Small Garden . . . Bitter Weed* (Morant Boy, Jamaica: Maroon Publishing House, 1980). See also Norman Girvan, "Aspects of the Political Economy of Race in the Caribbean and the Americas: A Preliminary Interpretation," Working Paper no. 7 (Mona, Jamaica: ISER, 1975).

7. Preston E. James, "Man-Land Relations in the Caribbean Area," in *Caribbean Studies: A Symposium* (Seattle and London: University of Washington Press, 1957), p. 1.

8. Edward Kamau Braithwaite, *Contradictory Omens: Cultural Diversity and Integration in the Caribbean,* Monograph no. 1 (Port of Spain, Trinidad: Savacou Publications, 1974), p. 28.

9. Ibid., p. 29.

10. Girvan, "Aspects of the Political Economy of Race," pp. 4–6.

11. Ibid., pp. 7–8.

12. George Beckford, "Peasant Movements and Agrarian Problems in the West Indies," *Caribbean Quarterly* 18 (March 1972):47.

13. Woodville K. Marshall, "Notes on Peasant Development in the West Indies Since 1838," in *Selected Papers from the Third West Indian Agricultural Economics Conference* (St. Augustine, Trinidad: University of the West Indies [UWI], 1968), p. 252.

14. Ibid.; see also Woodville K. Marshall, "Peasant Movements and Agrarian Problems in the West Indies: Aspects of the Development of the Peasantry," *Caribbean Quarterly* 18 (March 1972):31.

15. C. Y. Shephard, *Peasant Agriculture in the Leeward and Windward Islands* (St. Augustine, Trinidad: UWI, Imperial College of Tropical Agriculture, 1945), p. 2.

16. Ibid., p. 2.

17. Ibid., p. 3. See also Marshall, "Peasant Movements and Agrarian Problems," p. 31.

18. Marshall, "Peasant Movements and Agrarian Problems," p. 31.

19. Marshall, "Notes on Peasant Development," p. 259.

20. Beckford, "Peasant Movements," p. 47.

21. Marshall, "Notes on Peasant Development," pp. 261–262.

22. Shephard, *Peasant Agriculture,* p. 4.

23. Marshall, "Notes on Peasant Development," p. 262; Shephard, *Peasant Agriculture,* p. 4.

24. Shephard, *Peasant Agriculture,* pp. 4, 13–15.

25. Marshall, "Notes on Peasant Development," p. 263.

26. Ibid., p. 262.

27. Marshall, "Peasant Movements and Agrarian Problems," p. 37.

28. Ibid., p. 34.

29. L. E. Braithwaite, "Social and Political Aspects of Rural Development in the West Indies," in *Selected Papers from the Third West Indian Agricultural Economics Conference* (St. Augustine, Trinidad: UWI, 1968), p. 273.

30. Ibid.

31. E. R. St. J. Cumberbatch, "Man and the Land in the Caribbean," paper prepared for the International Rural Development Conference (Montreal: McGill University, McDonald College, 1976), p. 1.

32. Lewis G. Campbell, "Strategy for Maximising Self-Sufficiency in Food in the Region," in *Proceedings of the Tenth West Indies Agricultural Economics Conference* (St. Augustine, Trinidad: UWI, 1975), p. 56.

33. See Hamid O'Brien, "The Competition for Resources (Especially Labour and Land) Between the Oil Industry and Agriculture in Trinidad and Tobago," *Proceedings of the Ninth West Indian Agricultural Economics Conference* (St. Augustine, Trinidad: UWI, 1974), p. 197. See also T.M.A. Farrell and O. M. Nurse, "Oil and Agriculture in the Economic Development of Trinidad and Tobago: Competition or Symbiosis," *Proceedings of the Ninth West Indian Agricultural Economics Conference* (St. Augustine, Trinidad: UWI, 1974), p. 117.

34. Headley A. Brown, "The Impact of the Tourist Industries on the Agricultural Sectors—The Case of Jamaica," *Proceedings of the Ninth West Indian Agricultural Economics Conference* (St. Augustine, Trinidad: UWI, 1974), p. 131; V. G. Hill and S. A. Williams, "The Relationship Between the Bauxite Industry and the Agricultural Sector in Jamaica," *Proceedings of the Ninth West Indian Agricultural Economics Conference* (St. Augustine, Trinidad: UWI, 1974), p. 94; J. W. Phillips and J. L. Dukhia, "The Competition for Resources (Especially Land and Labour) Between Extractive Industries and Agriculture: The Case of Guyana's Bauxite Industry," *Proceedings of the Ninth West Indian Agricultural Economics Conference* (St. Augustine, Trinidad: UWI, 1974), pp. 101–104.

35. John M. Bryden, "The Impact of the Tourist Industries on the Agricultural Sectors: The Competition for Resources and Food Demand Aspects," *Proceedings of the Ninth West Indian Agricultural Economics Conference* (St. Augustine, Trinidad: UWI, 1974), p. 154; Janet D. Momsen, "Report on Vegetable Production and the Tourist Industry in Montserrat," mimeo (Calgary, Alberta: University of Calgary Press, 1973), p. 45.

36. E. Floto, *Agrarian Dualism in a Non-Agricultural Economy*, Working Paper no. 29 (Cambridge, England: University of Cambridge, Centre of Latin American Studies, 1977), p. 5.

37. E.R. St. J. Cumberbatch, "Prospects for Caribbean Agriculture," paper prepared for the Second Caribbean Seminar on Scientific and Technological Planning (St. Augustine, Trinidad: UWI, 1976) p. iii.

38. Ibid., p. 5.

39. Ibid., p. 7.

40. Ibid., p. 9.

41. IBRD/IDA, *Caribbean Regional Study*, vol. 3, p. 5; Caribbean Development Bank (CDB), *Small Farming in the Less Developed Countries of the Commonwealth Caribbean*, report prepared by Weir's Agricultural Consulting Service, Jamaica (Barbados: CDB, 1980), pp. 319–321.

42. Curtis E. McIntosh and Michael Lim Choy, *The Performance of Selected Agricultural Marketing Agencies*, Occasional Series no. 11 (St. Augustine, Trinidad: UWI, Department of Agricultural Economics and Farm Management, 1975), pp. 3–4.

43. K. A. Leslie, "Contribution of Agriculture to Economic Development—A Case Study of the West Indies: 1950–1963," *Proceedings of the First West Indian Agricultural Economics Conference* (St. Augustine, Trinidad: UWI, 1967), p. 12.

44. Cumberbatch, "Prospects for Caribbean Agriculture," p. iii.

45. IBRD/IDA, *Caribbean Regional Study*, vol. 3, pp. i, 1.

46. United Nations (UN)/ECLA, Office for the Caribbean, *Economic Activity 1979 in Caribbean Countries*, CEPAL/CARIB 80/5 (Port of Spain, Trinidad: UN, 1980), p. IV-11; UN/ECLA, *Economic Activities 1981 in Caribbean Countries*, CEPAL/CARIB 82/10 (Port of Spain, Trinidad: UN, 1982), p. XI-3.

47. Ibid., pp. IV-4, 5; XI-3.

48. Ibid., p. IV-2. For a detailed analysis of the agricultural sector in Trinidad and Tobago, see Republic of Trinidad and Tobago, Ministry of Agriculture, Lands, and Fisheries, *White Paper on Agriculture* (Port of Spain, Trinidad: Government Printery, 1979). See also E. Floto, *Agrarian Dualism in a Non-Agricultural Economy*; Farrell and Nurse, "Oil and Agriculture in the Economic Development of Trinidad and Tobago," pp. 117–126.

49. UN/ECLA, *Economic Activity 1979 in Caribbean Countries*, pp. VII-4, 5; UN/ECLA, *Economic Activities 1981 in Caribbean Countries*, p. IX-3.

50. UN/ECLA, *Economic Activity 1979 in Caribbean Countries*, p. VII-8. For an analysis of the agricultural sector in Jamaica, see I. E. Johnson and M. O. Strachan, "Agricultural Development in Jamaica," *Proceedings of*

the *Ninth West Indian Agricultural Economics Conference* (St. Augustine, Trinidad: UWI, 1974), pp. 3–20. See also Owen Jefferson, *The Post-War Economic Development of Jamaica* (Mona, Jamaica: ISER, 1972), pp. 72–124; K. A. Leslie and L. B. Rankine, "Food Supplies in the Commonwealth Caribbean: The Case of Jamaica," *Proceedings of the Tenth West Indies Agricultural Economics Conference* (St. Augustine, Trinidad: UWI, 1975), pp. 23–37.

51. UN/ECLA, *Economic Activity 1979 in Caribbean Countries*, pp. III-1–3; UN/ECLA, *Economic Activities 1981 in Caribbean Countries*, p. IV-3.

52. UN/ECLA, *Economic Activity 1981 in Caribbean Countries*, p. III-4; p. IV-3.

53. Ibid., p. III-15; p. IV-3. For an analysis of the agricultural sector of Barbados, see Government of Barbados, Ministry of Finance and Planning, *Barbados Development Plan 1979–83: Planning for Growth* (Bridgetown, Barbados: Government Printing Office, 1980), pp. 57–70. See also E. C. Pilgrim, "The Role and Structure of Agriculture in Barbados and the Agricultural Development Programme," *Proceedings of the Fourth West Indian Agricultural Economics Conference* (St. Augustine, Trinidad: UWI, 1969), pp. 55–66; F. Alleyne, "The Expansion of Tourism and Its Concomitant Unrealised Potential for Agricultural Development in the Barbadian Economy," *Proceedings of the Ninth West Indian Agricultural Economics Conference* (St. Augustine, Trinidad: UWI, 1974), pp. 143–152.

54. UN/ECLA, *Economic Activity 1979 in Caribbean Countries*, p. VI-3; UN/ECLA, *Economic Activity 1981 in Caribbean Countries*, p. VIII-5.

55. UN/ECLA, *Economic Activity 1979 in Caribbean Countries*, p. VI-4; UN/ECLA, *Economic Activity 1981 in Caribbean Countries*, p. VIII-6. For a more detailed analysis of recent economic developments in Guyana, including those in agriculture, see International Bank for Reconstruction and Development (IBRD), *Economic Memorandum on Guyana*, Report no. 3015-GUA (Washington, D.C.: IBRD, 1980). See also Government of Guyana, Ministry of Agriculture, *Crop and Livestock Statistics in Guyana: A Compilation of Existing Data* (Georgetown, Guyana: Inter-American Institute of Agricultural Sciences, 1980); Bonham C. Richardson, "Guyana's 'Green Revolution': Social and Ecological Problems in the Agricultural Development Programme," *Caribbean Quarterly* 18 (March 1972):14–23; Bonham C. Richardson, "The Agricultural Dilemma of the Post-Plantation Caribbean," *Inter-American Economic Affairs* 26 (Summer 1972):59–70.

56. See Government of Belize, Ministry of Natural Resources, Department of Agriculture, *A Summary of Statistics 1979* (Belmopan, Belize: Government Printers, 1980); Government of Belize, Central Planning Unit, *Economic Plan of Belize 1980–1983* (Belmopan, Belize: Government Printers, 1980). See also International Bank for Reconstruction and Development, *Economic Memorandum on Belize*, Report no. 2909-BEL (Washington, D.C.: IBRD, 1980); UN/ECLA, *Economic Activity 1981 in Caribbean Countries*, p. V-4.

57. Caribbean Development Bank, *Small Farming in the Less Developed Countries of the Commonwealth Caribbean*, p. 312.

58. Ibid., p. 318. For more detailed analysis on the economic situation in St. Vincent, see International Bank for Reconstruction and Development, *Economic Memorandum on St. Vincent and the Grenadines,* Report no. 2935-CRG (Washington, D.C.: IBRD, 1980). On Grenada, see UN/ECLA, Office for the Caribbean, *Agricultural Sector Plan for Grenada 1977–1981,* ECLA/CARIB77/3 (Port of Spain, Trinidad: ECLA, 1977). See also International Bank for Reconstruction and Development, *Economic Memorandum on Grenada,* Report no. 2949-GRD (Washington, D.C.: IBRD, 1980); UN/ECLA, *Report on a Farm Survey Conducted in Grenada,* CEPAL/CARIB79/12 (Port of Spain, Trinidad: ECLA, 1979).

59. Caribbean Development Bank, *Small Farming in the Less Developed Countries of the Commonwealth Caribbean,* p. 318. See also International Bank for Reconstruction and Development, *Economic Memorandum on St. Kitts-Nevis,* Report no. 2948-CRG (Washington, D.C.: IBRD, 1980); International Bank for Reconstruction and Development, *Economic Memorandum on Dominica,* Report no. 2923-CRG (Washington, D.C.: IBRD, 1980).

60. UN/ECLA, *Economic Activity 1979 in Caribbean Countries,* p. VIII-7.

61. See Caribbean Development Bank, *Small Farming in the Less Developed Countries of the Commonwealth Caribbean,* chs. 6 and 7. For details on the agricultural sector in Montserrat, see Government of Montserrat, *Five Year Draft Plan 1979–1983: Agricultural Sector* (Plymouth, Montserrat: 1980); International Bank for Reconstruction and Development, *Economic Memorandum on Montserrat,* Report no. 2943-MO (Washington, D.C.: IBRD, 1980). On Antigua, see International Bank for Reconstruction and Development, *Economic Memorandum on Antigua,* Report no. 2928-CRG (Washington, D.C.: IBRD, 1980).

62. Sidney Chernick, *The Commonwealth Caribbean: The Integration Experience* (Baltimore and London: Johns Hopkins University Press, 1978), p. 118.

63. Ibid., p. 119.

64. International Bank for Reconstruction and Development, *Regional Agricultural Development and Food Production in the Caribbean,* Report no. 2064-CRB (Washington, D.C.: IBRD, 1978), p. 5; CARICOM Secretariat, "Towards the Development of the Agricultural Sector of the Caribbean Community: The Regional Food Plan and the Regional Food and Nutrition Strategy," *CARICOM Bulletin,* no. 3 (1982):10–18.

65. Chernick, *The Commonwealth Caribbean,* p. 121.

66. International Bank for Reconstruction and Development, *Regional Agricultural Development and Food Production in the Caribbean,* p. 5. For more detailed information on nutrition in the Caribbean, see J. M. Gurney, "Available Data on the State of Food and Nutrition of the Peoples of the Commonwealth Caribbean," *Proceedings of the Tenth West Indies Agricultural Economics Conference* (St. Augustine, Trinidad: UWI, 1975), pp. 66–75. See also Jacques M. May and Donna L. McLellan, "The Ecology of Malnutrition in the Caribbean," *Studies in Medical Geography,* vol. 12 (New York: Hafner Press, 1973).

67. Johnson and Strachan, "Agricultural Development in Jamaica," p. 12; Leslie and Rankine, "Food Supplies in the Commonwealth Caribbean," pp. 29–30.

68. Government of Trinidad and Tobago, *White Paper on Agriculture*, p. 32.

69. IBRD/IDA, *Caribbean Regional Study*, Vol. 3, p. 3.

5
Agricultural Policy in the Caribbean: A Regional Response

The serious problems facing food production in the Caribbean are not new to the region. Although size, climate, topography, and geology all contribute to these difficulties, their roots lie in the economic and political history of the region. Perhaps most discouraging is the fact that although the problems have been recognized for a long time, there has been little success in improving conditions, and now the situation has reached crisis proportions. A number of reasons underlie the inadequacy of national policies; two of the most important are limited resources and an excessive emphasis on industrialization as the path to development.

At the regional level, the integration effort has been concerned primarily with industrialization, agriculture having originally been given a relatively low priority in CARIFTA, mainly as a distributive measure to provide benefits for the LDCs. In the time since the integration movement stalled in the mid-1970s, CARICOM has undertaken new initiatives in the agricultural sector. In taking these initiatives CARICOM has moved agriculture from a position of low priority, where it was seen as instrumental and secondary to achieving trade integration in manufactures, to a position of high priority, where development of the food sector has become a principal aim in itself.

By looking at the evolution of integration policy within the agricultural sector, we can observe a pattern that reflects the larger tendency of regional integration to move toward more *dirigiste* solutions to problems. This evolution also reflects a shift toward greater concern for satisfaction of basic needs.[1] The thrust of regional policy in the agricultural sector in the Caribbean has changed from one limited to individual sectoral agreements for specific commodities (rice, and oils and fats) to a comprehensive framework of integrated planning across the entire regional food and nutrition sector. The major elements of this policy include the Rice Agreements and the

Oils and Fats Agreement, which predated the establishment of CAR-IFTA in 1968; the Agriculture Marketing Protocol (AMP) and its modifications, including the Guaranteed Market Scheme (GMS); the Regional Food Plan, originally conceived as a major effort to achieve food self-sufficiency, and now the Regional Food and Nutrition Strategy, reflecting the broad concern with satisfying basic needs; and, finally, a number of research and financial programs designed to help increase food production in the region.

In addition to the Standing Committee of Ministers Responsible for Agriculture, which formulates policy in the agricultural sector, institutions that have been active in the implementation of regional agricultural policy are the Caribbean Investment Corporation (CIC), formally abolished in 1983; the Caribbean Development Bank (CDB); and the Caribbean Food Corporation (CFC). Taken together, these regional efforts in the agricultural sector in the Caribbean represent the most ambitious policies among all integration schemes in developing areas to solve some of the major difficulties in meeting local basic needs in foodstuffs. The development of Caribbean regional agricultural policy reflects the adaptation and evolution of regional integration as a strategy for development within the constraints of dependent underdevelopment in a changing global economy.

In the early stages of Caribbean integration, regional agricultural policy reflected the minimalist *laissez-faire* approach characteristic of the beginnings of CARIFTA. As Caribbean integration deepened and the shortcomings of this approach became apparent, measures taken in the agricultural sector reflected a change in thinking. More *dirigiste* policies were envisaged, and steps were taken toward more intensive integration within the agricultural sector.

The CARIFTA Agreement came into force on May 1, 1968, as did the Agriculture Marketing Protocol (AMP), which provided for protected regional trade with respect to twenty-two selected regionally produced agricultural commodities.[2] The AMP constituted the extension and incorporation into a regional integration scheme of the principles that had been applied through subsectoral agreements for two commodities: rice, and oils and fats. The Rice Agreements and the Oils and Fats Agreement originally came in force during World War II. In the case of rice, Guyana had three separate agreements: one with the Windward Islands, Leeward Islands, and Barbados; one with Jamaica; and one with Trinidad and Tobago. Under these agreements, Guyana would supply, at an agreed price, all the rice required by these territories, which in turn would agree to purchase only from Guyana unless the latter was unable to satisfy their needs.[3]

The Oils and Fats Agreement pertained to all CARIFTA member territories except Jamaica and the Leeward Islands. It was substantially revised in 1970 and redrafted as a protocol to the CARIFTA Agreement, and its membership was extended to include all CARIFTA territories. The Oils and Fats Agreement provided for the fixing of area export prices of copra and raw and refined oil; for the allocation of markets on the basis of declarations of surpluses and deficits of copra by member territories; and for the control of imports of oils, fats, and substitutes from outside the area. The effect was to guarantee export prices and markets for both the raw materials and the semimanufactured products.[4]

The Agricultural Marketing Protocol:
A Market Approach

The subsectoral agreements in rice and oils and fats provided the background and experience for the adoption of the Agricultural Marketing Protocol as part of the CARIFTA Agreement—a first attempt to include agriculture within the larger context of regional integration. As an integrative measure, the AMP was seen both as a means to create net benefits for the region within the agricultural sector and as a means to redress the unequal gains from integration in the industrial sector, by creating benefits for the mainly agricultural LDCs.

The establishment of the AMP represented the first concrete measure in the move toward rationalization of the regional agricultural sector. Although CARIFTA set forth no detailed policy outline for agricultural rationalization, the goal of rationalization is implicit in Articles 17:4(a) and 18:7(a) of the CARIFTA Agreement.[5] The CARICOM Treaty, on the other hand, contains an explicit commitment to the rationalization of agricultural production, including these specific objectives:

1. The development of a regional plan for the integration of agricultural development
2. Achievement of the optimum utilization of agricultural resources
3. Improvement of the efficiency of agricultural production
4. Import substitution on a regional basis
5. Increasing the income and standard of living of the rural population
6. Contributing to the achievement of full employment
7. Provision of greater opportunities to the LDCs for expansion of agricultural exports within and outside the region.[6]

As its name indicates, the AMP represented a market-oriented solution to problems in the agricultural sector. Its conception reflects a logical transferal of the idea of integration as a region-wide form of import substitution to the agricultural sector. The AMP designated a list of regionally produced foodstuffs that (1) offered some scope for expansion of production, (2) were imported into the region in significant quantities, and (3) possessed an export capacity on the part of certain member territories. The AMP aimed to regulate trade in these foodstuffs by allocating intraregional production according to surpluses and deficits declared by the member countries, and by prohibiting extraregional imports of these products and near substitutes when regional supplies were available. Market allocations were proportionately specified for each commodity among member territories based on estimated surpluses and deficits, with prices fixed at semi-annual meetings at a level designed to provide adequate returns to producers and a reasonable price to consumers.[7]

In short, the AMP was conceived to encourage agricultural development of the Caribbean region as a whole by ensuring that commodities capable of being produced in the area were in fact produced and distributed, and to create special benefits for those LDCs in the region in which small farming contributes a larger proportion to the GDP.[8] But it is not surprising that the original policy instrument used to implement the goal of rationalization of the agricultural sector was essentially a mechanism to create a system of modified free trade. The AMP simply reflected the larger thrust of the Caribbean integration movement in the direction of *laissez-faire* phased freeing of trade. As a marketing agreement, essentially, the AMP made no provision for regulating agricultural production in the region.[9]

It is clear that the Agricultural Marketing Protocol did not live up to expectations that it would stimulate the flow of intraregional trade, particularly from the LDCs to the MDCs, although it was perceived to be a limited success up until 1972.[10] The implementation of its procedures proved to be quite complex in practice, and they served to accentuate some of the shortcomings of the policy as well as to draw attention to conditions in the member countries that impeded its effective operation.

The promotion of intraregional trade under the AMP depended upon knowledge of basic supply and demand conditions in the region so that efficient allocation could be made. But this knowledge simply was not available because of the absence of reliable data on production and consumption in the countries of the region. Moreover, where data might have been available, trade could be allocated only when the surpluses and deficits were officially declared to the Secretariat and could be matched up. Often deficits were not declared, even though member countries were importing from third countries while declared surpluses existed in the region.

In addition, member countries were free under the provisions of the AMP to expand production in any of the commodities on the list in response to an increase in local demand and/or higher prices. Because the AMP price tended to be higher than the preexisting local price in many countries (especially the MDCs) and because the MDCs have a larger resource base on which to expand production, the AMP had the effect of stimulating production in the MDCs, thus thwarting both the goal of increasing regional trade and the goal of benefiting the LDCs.[11] Even after such minor changes as giving LDC surpluses priority over MDC surpluses and improving the means of communicating surpluses and deficits, the system was subject to serious criticism.

In response to such criticism, in July 1972 the Council of Ministers set up the Guaranteed Market Scheme (GMS), under which the MDCs were required to purchase selected commodities at AMP prices.[12] The MDCs undertook to accept specific quantities of these commodities each year, and to take whatever national measures were necessary to ensure that their capacity to absorb this production was not affected. The LDCs undertook to produce the crops to meet their commitments, thus ensuring that they would receive annual increments in the amounts purchased. Moreover, the MDCs agreed to provide technical assistance to help the LDCs meet their commitments under the agreement.[13]

Although some successes were recorded in trade under the AMP (notably, carrots produced in St. Vincent and tomatoes produced in Montserrat), little increase occurred in total production and intraregional trade.[14] St. Vincent was the only member territory to have experienced a continued increase over the period 1969–1973, when other LDCs were unable to meet their monthly commitments. Under the GMS, no LDC other than St. Vincent was able to supply carrots from November 1972 to April 1973. St. Vincent is often cited as a great success story, given its increase in production from 8,025 pounds in 1969 to 7.4 million pounds in 1976,[15] although by 1980 production had fallen back greatly.

It is now clear that the AMP/GMS led neither to the anticipated increases in regional trade in foodstuffs nor to increased markets for LDC products. A number of operational and organizational aspects of the AMP and GMS have been identified as contributing to the failure of the schemes to create the expected benefits, including the pricing system, the method of allocating surpluses and deficits, the role of marketing boards, payment difficulties, inadequate shipping facilities, poor quality control, and inefficient administration of the protocol.[16] More important, however, experience under the AMP/GMS has clearly demonstrated the mistaken assumption underlying the scheme: that given adequate market opportunities, increased agricultural production would be forthcoming. Given the overall *laissez-faire* thrust of the Caribbean integration movement, it is not surprising that the agricultural program was preoccupied with trade rather than production. Its failure starkly revealed obstacles to agricultural production in the region that are based in conditions much more deeply rooted than the simple lack of an organized market.[17] These structural problems pose great obstacles to agricultural development and require solutions more fundamental than those contained in the AMP/GMS. In July 1983, it was agreed that the Agricultural Marketing Protocol as a mechanism for facilitating intraregional trade in agricultural products would be abolished, but that existing arrangements would continue until new ones could be put into effect.

Agricultural conditions in the Caribbean are historically rooted in the colonial experience of plantation agriculture discussed in the preceding chapter and have been extensively analyzed by scholars in the region.[18] Emphasis has been placed by governments on the development of traditional export crops, to the detriment of small-farmer cultivation of foodstuffs.[19] Domestic agriculture has been marked by fragmented holdings on poor land of declining fertility, resulting in low output and high production costs and in a low level of technology, skills, capital input, and research and credit facilities for nonplantation crops. It has also been handicapped by an irrational wage and price structure in an inadequate marketing system and a declining small-farm population of increasing age trying to survive in a society lacking social facilities in rural areas. This situation, in turn, has led to an unfavorable attitude toward agricultural work on the part of the West Indian population.[20]

The policies of the national governments in the region have done little to overcome the serious problems confronting the domestic food-producing sector. Development efforts in the industrial sector have taken precedence over domestic agriculture; accordingly, given the strong intersectoral competition for scarce land, there has been inadequate planning of land use.[21] Foreign capital flowing into the industrial and tourist sectors has led to the spilling over of inflated wages into the agricultural sector. At the same time, relatively few new employment opportunities have been created, resulting in both high unemployment and labor shortages in the agricultural sector.[22]

The existence of fundamental structural obstacles to development of local agriculture in combination with inadequate national policies for attacking these problems has inevitably led to a continued stagnation and decline in food production and an increasing food import bill. Given the limited scope and objectives of the regional agricultural policy as embodied in the AMP/GMS, there was little likelihood that it would have much impact on regional production.

By 1974, the Caribbean food deficit had reached crisis proportions, with an annual food import bill for that year of US$500 million and rising to US$800 million by 1980.[23] Major increases in energy costs and declining production in the traditional export sector led to a deteriorating balance of payments in the region (with the exception of Trinidad and Tobago). The rising food deficit and deteriorating balance of payments underlined the need to embark on a major effort to restructure the domestic agricultural sector on a regional basis, and to do so through policies directed at the basic problems on the production side rather than through policies limited to market solutions.

Toward Regional Sectoral Programming: Integration of Production

Within the regional integration movement in the Caribbean, the measures adopted to effect structural transformation of the agricultural sector range from *laissez-faire* policies to encourage greater output, on the one hand, to the creation of a regional public corporation with the power to engage in production, trade, and a wide range of other activities designed to contribute directly to agricultural development, on the other hand. The various elements of Caribbean agricultural policy can be grouped broadly into three categories: measures to provide credit for agricultural production, measures to provide for better use of agricultural inputs, and measures to program regional food production to respond to regional needs.

Agricultural Credit: The Role of the CDB

The Caribbean Development Bank (CDB), though not formally a CARICOM institution, has increasingly come to fill the role of a regional integration bank. The decision to create the CDB was taken at the 1967 Georgetown meetings when the CARIFTA Agreement was negotiated, and it has always been regarded by the LDCs of the region as a major mechanism of benefit to them. Data on the distribution of CDB financing confirms this view. The LDCs of the region have received nearly three-fourths (70.6 percent) of the "soft loans" granted by the bank and a total of 54.2 percent of the total net financing over the period 1970–1983. The financing for this period totals US$463.5 million, with "soft" financing constituting 63.4 percent of that total, or US$293.7 million.[24]

The importance of agriculture among the priorities of the CDB is reflected in the fact that from 1970 to 1980 nearly one-fourth (25.8 percent) of the total financing went to the agricultural sector—second only to the amount devoted to infrastructure (34.1 percent).[25] These figures include equity investment and loans (both direct and indirect) to private and public borrowers, as well as export and domestic agriculture. The oft-heard criticisms of the operation of the CDB, its stringent lending criteria, and the long delays between approvals and disbursement were well-founded in the case of financing small-farmer food production. Small farmers are among the potential recipients of CDB funds with the lowest net worth and are the least able either to meet the complex application procedures or to withstand the protracted delays in disbursement.

To respond more effectively to the particular needs of local food producers in the region, the CDB established the Farm Improvement Credit (FIC) scheme. This scheme, an agricultural fund financed by Canada, provides loans of EC$3,000 to EC$100,000 on a medium- to long-term basis at concessionary rates. The loans, which require collateral, are aimed at upgrading agricultural production. They are not directly granted to the farmer by the CDB but, rather, are administered through the intermediary of the Development Finance Corporation (DFC, sometimes called the Agricultural Development Bank) of each of the member territories. In addition to providing the funds to be reloaned by the DFCs, the CDB finances a Farm Improvement Officer, who is attached to the DFC to assist small farmers in preparing applications for the loans, to administer the loans, and to offer advice as to their best use. All of the LDCs of CARICOM and the British Virgin Islands are participants in the FIC program, which from 1970 to 1983 had disbursed a total of US$7.9 million out of $8.7 million dollars approved for thirty-three loans in the ten territories involved.[26] Data on approvals and disbursements of loans under the FIC program are provided in Table 5.1.

The FIC scheme has resulted in neither as large a number of projects nor as great an amount of financing as had been hoped, and eight of the approved loans representing nearly half the total financing have gone to projects in Belize. From these data it is clear that the small farmers in the Eastern Caribbean have not been able to call upon the resources of the CDB to the degree that had been expected.

Table 5.1

Total Approvals and Disbursements Under the Farm Improvement Credit Scheme
of the Caribbean Development Bank at December 31, 1983

($US '000)

| | Lines of Credit Approved 1970-1983 | | Sub-Loans Approved | | | | Amounts Disbursed | |
| | | | No. | | Amount | | | |
	No.	Amount	1983	1970-83	1983	1970-83	1983	1970-83
Antigua	3	655	10	111	39	793	49	774
Belize	8	3,858	50	511	352	3,852	267	3,276
British Virgin Islands	3	500	0	79	0	442	100	400
Cayman Islands	1	313	2	7	113	283	94	264
Dominica	4	1,244	47	491	144	1,294	144	1,231
Grenada	3	585	31	122	142	585	135	512
Montserrat	2	217	0	11	0	84	0	84
St. Kitts-Nevis	2	234	0	8	0	9	0	159
St. Lucia	4	1,077	56	704	173	865	64	700
St. Vincent	3	803	10	80	29	481	23	475
Total	33	9,486	206	2,124	992	8,688	876	7,875

SOURCE: Caribbean Development Bank, Annual Report 1983 (Bridgetown, Barbados: CDB, 1984), p. 54.

The reasons for this failure are of concern to the CDB and have been the subject of study on its part. Even given the concessionary rates and small size of the FIC loans, small farmers of the Eastern Caribbean have not been able either to meet the lending criteria or, in many cases, to initiate application procedures. Major problems with the administration of the loans through the DFCs have also become apparent, including problems with collecting outstanding debts.[27] As a result of these difficulties, a special division of the Caribbean Development Bank was set up to assist the DFCs in administering the indirect CDB loans.

Recognizing the need to make access to agricultural credit easier for the small farmer, the CDB established the Agricultural Production Credit (APC) scheme in 1977. This scheme, which expired in 1982, was aimed at overcoming the major deficiency of short-term production credit, which DFCs and local governments had difficulty satisfying through their own resources. Using soft funds provided by the United States Agency for International Development (USAID), the APC program granted short-term loans (up to eighteen months) ranging from US$200 to US$4,000 to small farmers in the LDCs. As in the FIC scheme, these funds were loaned by the CDB indirectly through the local DFCs; but they were also subject to less restrictive conditions than those associated with the FIC loans, requiring only a crop lien as collateral. The objective of the APC program was to allow the small farmer to upgrade production by purchasing seeds, fertilizer, pesticides, and other agricultural inputs. Although the APC was designed to provide greater access to Caribbean Development Bank financing for local food production, problems with administration of the loans by the local financial institutions still remained, particularly with regard to reducing the degree of defaulting and arrears in repayment. By the end of 1983, a total of US$2.3 million in loans had been approved and US$1.9 million had been disbursed.[28] Data on the approval and disbursement of loans under the APC are provided in Table 5.2.

For larger projects the CDB provides direct loans, in both export and local agriculture, although its emphasis is on increasing local food production. The bank has evolved from its earlier *laissez-faire* approach of providing financing toward a more active promotion of projects through the initiation of studies, provision of technical assistance, and direct equity participation with governments in specific subsectors in which it believes a need exists.

In addition to agricultural project assistance funded through the agricultural section of the bank, the CDB finances agricultural feeder roads through the infrastructure section and agro-industry through

Table 5.2

Total Approvals and Disbursements Under the Agricultural Production Credit Scheme of the Caribbean Development Bank at December 31, 1983
($US '000)

| | Lines of Credit Approved 1970-1983 | | Sub-Loans Approved | | | | | |
| | | | No. | | Amount | | Amounts Disbursed | |
	No.	Amount	1983	1970-83	1983	1970-83	1983	1970-83
Antigua	1	192	0	237	0	239	0	166
Belize	1	1,245	0	1,296	0	1,245	0	1,027
British Virgin Islands	0	0	0	0	0	0	0	0
Cayman Islands[a]	1	187	0	0	0	0	0	0
Dominica	1	181	44	214	44	225	32	198
Grenada[b]	1	222	59	299	21	164	21	121
Montserrat	0	0	0	0	0	0	0	0
St. Kitts-Nevis	0	0	0	0	0	0	0	0
St. Lucia	1	397	0	406	0	390	0	345
St. Vincent	0	0	0	0	0	0	0	0
Total	6	2,424	103	2,452	65	2,263	53	1,857

SOURCE: Caribbean Development Bank, Annual Report 1983 (Bridgetown, Barbados: CDB, 1984), p. 54.

a Loan cancelled.
b $102,000 cancelled.

the industrial projects section. Through these activities the Caribbean Development Bank has become a major source of agricultural credit in the region, although its impact on the production of local foodstuffs by the small farmer has not yet been significant.

Although inadequate agricultural credit facilities may be an obstacle to the transformation of the local food production sector, as is the lack of an adequate marketing system, the availability of credit is not a sufficient condition to overcome the structural problems facing this sector. The available financial resources must be translated into productive activity through changes at the farm level—changes that require a direct approach to individual farmers and an expansion of production through the creation of new agricultural enterprises.

Research and Development: CARDI and CARDATS

The sad state of local food production in the Caribbean stems from centuries of neglect as a result of concentration on the production of traditional export crops—principally sugar, bananas, citrus, spices, cocoa, and coffee. The richest land, the most labor, the best technology, and the largest investments were directed to this subsector to the detriment of food production. As part of this policy, virtually all of the agricultural research in the region was devoted to increasing production in the export sector. More recently, following the political independence of many of the territories, scarce resources have been concentrated in the industrial sector, thus further contributing to the neglect of food production.

The result has been that small farmers producing food in the region are operating under the handicap of low farm-management skills, poor husbandry techniques, and inadequate agricultural inputs, which, in turn, have resulted in low levels of production, poor quality of produce, and reduced productivity. These conditions are particularly acute in the Eastern Caribbean, where governments have not responded to the needs of small farmers, often owing to the lack of resources on the part of these governments; but even in the larger countries of the region, policies on the national level—including agricultural extension services—have not greatly improved the situation.[29]

In response to these problems, a number of regional efforts have been undertaken in the area of agricultural research and development. The Caribbean Agricultural Research and Development Institute (CARDI) was established in 1975 as a regional institution to serve the research and development needs of the member countries of CARICOM. CARDI is the successor to the Regional Research Centre attached to the Imperial College of Tropical Agriculture dating from 1965 and is now a region-wide organization responsible to the Standing

Committee of the Ministers of Agriculture of CARICOM.[30] The core budget of CARDI is funded by the member countries of CARICOM, with Jamaica and the republic of Trinidad and Tobago each paying one-third of the budget, Barbados and Guyana one-ninth each, and the LDCs together providing the remaining one-ninth. Specific projects are funded by various donor agencies, including USAID, the European Development Fund (EDF), the Canadian International Development Agency (CIDA), the International Development Research Centre (IDRC), the CDB, the United Nations Development Program (UNDP), the Overseas Development Administration (ODA) of the United Kingdom, the Food and Agriculture Organization (FAO), and Barclay's Bank International.

The program of CARDI was developed in consultation with the Ministries of Agriculture of the member countries, the commodity organizations in the region, and various regional institutions as part of the effort to advance regional agricultural research and development. CARDI also serves as a means for coordinating external agricultural aid coming into the region and supplies the agricultural research and development needs of the LDCs, which cannot afford to undertake these activities on an individual basis. As the Regional Food and Nutrition Strategy progresses (see following section), CARDI will play a key role in providing technical assistance to it and its main implementing agency, the Caribbean Food Corporation.

The CARDI program includes commodity research aimed at removing constraints on the production of various crops or livestock, agricultural training geared to upgrading levels of expertise and introducing new methodologies and techniques, and dissemination of information to meet the needs of agricultural technicians and planners in the region.[31] Its efforts are directed toward applied research in agriculture, with pure research being left to the Faculty of Agriculture of the University of the West Indies (UWI).

Although these efforts cover the entire spectrum of agricultural production, including traditional export crops, increased local food production has been identified as the primary objective for the agricultural sector, and CARDI's main thrust has been to assist the small farmer in improving the farming system. The major program that brings the regional agricultural effort to the level of the individual small farmer is CARDI's Small Farm Multiple Cropping Program, a four-year renewable program funded by a USAID grant of US$4.5 million.

This program was begun in mid-1979 in the Leeward and Windward Islands as a combined field research and intervention project involving all parts of the farming system. It represents a departure from the traditional approach to agricultural research in the region, which develops data at an experimental station and then applies the results to actual small farms, often with little success. The Small Farm Multiple Cropping Program carries out research on a selected sample of farms under real farming conditions to see how farmers make day-to-day decisions. A research team monitors and gathers information weekly on all farm activities: planting, weeding, watering, household labor, hired labor, use of fertilizer and pesticides, distribution of livestock, yields, diseases, pests, and so on. Then, after about fourteen months of data gathering and analysis, direct intervention is commenced within the farming system based on the research. One farmer, for example, may be advised to plant legumes to improve his family's nutrition; another might be recommended to introduce new crop varieties or different methods of pest and disease control. CARDI supplies the inputs necessary for the intervention, and the results of the intervention, in turn, are then further researched.

The activities of the field officers of CARDI are designed to contribute to the education of members of a small number of farms; later, this learning is more generally applied through the "demonstration effect" of diffusion of knowledge within the farming community. Eventually, the results of the Small Farm Multiple Cropping Program will be integrated into a separate USAID-funded agricultural extension program for the Eastern Caribbean aimed at bringing the benefits of this agricultural knowledge to all small farmers of the region.

A subregional agricultural extension project is also being carried out by a separate program, the Caribbean Agricultural and Rural Development Advisory and Training Service (CARDATS), which is funded by UNDP and executed by the FAO. CARICOM is a cooperating agency of CARDATS but will eventually replace FAO as the executing agency. CARDATS is an integrated rural development program that provides direct services to small farmers relating to all aspects of farming, but without the preliminary research stage of CARDI's small-farm program. In effect, CARDATS aims to *create* small farmers in the eastern Caribbean where they never really existed as such, inasmuch as they more often work for wages in plantation agriculture and survive as marginal cultivators on small plots for subsistence and small trading.[32] CARDATS provides support and services in financing, marketing, supply of inputs, and knowledge of farm management on a direct day-to-day basis, and it works with a UN volunteer and a counterpart of the Agricultural Ministry in each of the eight territories (one in each of the ECCM countries, although Nevis has one of its own). It hopes through this training experience to demonstrate that small farmers can be well-off and enjoy a relatively comfortable life and, hence, to attract people to the land and begin to overcome the social repugnance toward agricultural work in the region.

Both CARDI and CARDATS represent regional efforts to bring about agricultural development through direct action at the individual level on the production side, thus reflecting an important advance beyond the *laissez-faire* regional market solution represented by the AMP. A further recognition of the need to pursue more direct policies to transform regional agriculture is found in the steps being taken toward the establishment of a program of regional planning in the agricultural sector.

The Regional Food and Nutrition Strategy and the CFC

By 1981 agricultural exports from the Commonwealth Caribbean were no longer sufficient to pay for extraregional food imports. By 1973 the regional food import bill was US$300 million, and by 1980 it had reached US$800 million. The starkness of these figures in a region that is predominantly agricultural provided a stimulus for more direct regional action to overcome the problem.[33] The late prime minister of Trinidad and Tobago, Eric Williams, had drawn attention to the need for region-wide efforts toward greater self-sufficiency, and steps were taken to begin development of a regional food plan.[34] These efforts have developed into a Regional Food and Nutrition Strategy for the Caribbean and the creation of the Caribbean Food Corporation (CFC), which has been described as "the greatest cooperative venture in the history of the Commonwealth Caribbean."[35]

The first steps toward these policies were taken at the CARICOM Heads of Government Meeting in St. Kitts in December 1975, at which a Working Party on Food Production submitted proposals for the establishment of a Regional Food Plan and Food Corporation. The general aims of this corporation were to maximize regional food production for local consumption by mobilizing unused and underutilized agricultural and other resources. High priority was given to increasing substantially the allocation of resources to food production in the Windward and Leeward Islands.[36]

The adoption of the Regional Food Plan reflected a shift in the approach to solving the problems of development of Caribbean agriculture from an essentially *laissez-faire* market approach to a *dirigiste* approach directed at restructuring agricultural production on a regional level. The AMP/GMS, as well as the regional efforts to provide agricultural credit and R&D, represent attempts to create the conditions for agricultural development, whereas the Regional Food Plan and the Caribbean Food Corporation envisage direct action by regional institutions to bring about this development.

The major issues addressed by the elaboration of the Regional Food Plan concern (1) the distribution of regional resources, given that Guyana and Belize have 90 percent of the land in the region and only 10 percent of the resources, and that the financial and technical resources are concentrated in the four MDCs; (2) the gearing of projects to satisfy national needs and priorities in such areas as employment and land use; and (3) the distribution of benefits by spreading the gains from combined operations among member countries. To respond to these requirements, the Regional Food Plan calls for a combining and sharing of resources across national boundaries, with a major role to be played by other regional institutions such as the CDB, CIC, CARDI, and ECCM, and the adoption of a phased project-by-project approach.[37]

Progress in implementing the Regional Food Plan has entailed preliminary design studies to assess production deficits for a number of subsectors and studies to determine production targets in member countries and the region as a whole; country programs to be worked out with each government, including prefeasibility studies subject to governmental approval; preparation of detailed feasibility studies once governmental approval has been granted, so that financial institutions (principally the CDB) can be approached for funding; and, finally, the actual carrying out of projects once financial arrangements have been devised.[38] A series of subsector projects identified for priority action are now in various stages of progress. These projects pertain to livestock, including milk and other dairy products, poultry, beef, mutton, and pork; fish and fish products; cereals, grain, and legumes; fruits and vegetables; spices and essential oils; agricultural inputs (including bulk purchasing); and oils and fats. Of these subsector projects, few have yet reached the implementation stage, although a number are in the study stage. Two large-scale grain projects, one in Guyana and one in Belize, have already harvested some crops, but both are undergoing modifications as a consequence of poor results.[39] Although progress on the subsector projects of the Regional Food Plan has not been as rapid as originally envisaged, significant developments have occurred since 1975 in other aspects of the plan.

In 1976, the Third Conference of Ministers Responsible for Agriculture took a decision to request the CARICOM secretary-general to broaden the thrust of the Regional Food Plan to cover the area of rural development, with an emphasis on productivity and the redistribution of income; measures to improve the combination, quality, and distribution of foodstuffs; and responsibility for health and other related activities.[40] In response to this request, which was endorsed by the Ministers Responsible for Health and for Education, the CARICOM Secretariat formulated a framework for a broad multisectoral food and nutrition policy for the Caribbean Community as a whole. In October 1979, a committee composed of the heads of regional and international agencies involved in food and nutrition agreed on the proposals and set up an Inter-Sectoral Committee (ISC) with a mandate to prepare a draft Food and Nutrition Strategy. This committee met in Barbados in October 1979 and August 1980, and produced a draft multisectoral plan covering agriculture, health, education, and communications entitled *CARICOM Feeds Itself: A Regional Food and Nutrition Strategy—A Strategy for the 80s.*[41] This working document represents the framework underlying both the major objectives of regional programming in agriculture and the programs that will be devised and implemented to achieve these objectives. It is to be carried out through a series of consultations within the regional community so that the document can be refined and priorities set before a proposal for implementation is put to the political directorate for its consideration.[42]

The CARICOM Regional Food and Nutrition Strategy has explicitly adopted the objective of providing for the basic needs of the society through sectoral programming across a broad range of activities.[43] The proposed strategy is composed of nine Program Areas scheduled over a period of ten years, with the following goals:

1. Increased production and availability of food, especially nutritionally important commodities.
2. Increased regional food reserves.
3. Increased consumption of nutritionally important food, especially by "at risk" groups (children and expectant mothers).
4. Improved health status of mothers and children in the region.
5. Reduced incidence of nutrition-related diseases.
6. Development of more relevant and effective education at school and adult levels, especially in the areas of agriculture, food and nutrition, and health sciences.
7. Development of more trained technical personnel.
8. Development of active support and public participation in the programs through a communications component.
9. Development of an effective organizational and management system for the strategy.[44]

The targets set by this basic-needs approach to the satisfaction of food and nutrition requirements are to provide from regional resources, by 1990, a minimum of 80 percent of the energy and 60 percent of the protein consumed in the region, and are to make available on a daily basis in the regional market the minimum recommended per capita dietary allowance of protein and energy in the appropriate protein/energy ratio.[45] The central focus of the strategy is collective action to achieve greater self-sufficiency and self-reliance in food through the restructuring of regional supplies to meet current and anticipated demand and/or the adjusting of regional consumption patterns to meet possible or potential supply.[46] This "integration of production" approach is spelled out in Program 1 of the Regional Food and Nutrition Strategy. Program 1 focuses on increased food production and availability made possible through measures in which land resources are allocated to the production of nutritionally important food to meet current and future demand, with consideration given to the need to maximize foreign exchange savings, net farm gate income, and employment.[47]

Five elements of this program can be identified.[48] The first element involves increased production of agricultural commodities (including fish products) for the local and export markets based on the provision of an effective agricultural extension service, adequate inputs to farmers (including seeds, feed, fertilizer, insecticides, and credit), more effective incentive schemes, and accelerated land reform programs and application of appropriate technology. The second element involves the reduction of post-harvest food losses through development of better techniques for identifying these losses, improvements in pest and disease control, and improvements in methods of harvesting, handling, and presale sorting and in appropriate storage facilities. The third element involves the creation of an adequate marketing infrastructure to bring about an increase in the quantity and quality of food available though improvement of the capacity and efficiency of public marketing agencies; establishment of effective market information systems; improvements in the food transportation system; provision of ancillary services such as market research, development, and promotion; improvement of facilities available to small traders; and improvement in regulations affecting trade in agricultural commodities, including the AMP. The fourth element involves an amelioration of the food-processing infrastructure, with an emphasis on determination of appropriate processing technologies (specifically, those that are multipurpose and adapted to local resources), training of skilled personnel, increased food fortification, and establishment of physical facilities on a rational basis to increase processing capacity. Finally, the fifth element involves the increased production of export crops to provide foreign exchange for production inputs and nonlocal food imports.

The measures identified for this last area include increasing the efficiency of production through appropriate technology, increasing the stability of the export market, and increasing the labor supply to the agricultural sector.

These five elements constitute the broad outline of a sectoral program to increase food self-reliance and self-sufficiency within the larger Regional Food and Nutrition Strategy. The goals and means of the strategy are extremely ambitious, and their realization will depend, *inter alia,* upon the creation of a complex organizational structure involving a series of regional and national institutions in the areas of food, nutrition, health, and education.[49] It should be emphasized that the Food and Nutrition Strategy is still in the formulation stage, with approval of its general thrust and specific programs yet to be formally adopted and full implementation even further in the future. The implementation stage has been reached, however, in the subsectoral projects identified in the earlier Regional Food Plan, and the major implementing agency, the Caribbean Food Corporation (CFC), has actually begun operation. The CFC provides an excellent example of the kind of direct intervention that will be needed to bring about the restructuring of agricultural production in the region.

The Caribbean Food Corporation was proposed at the same time the Working Party in Food Production submitted the Regional Food Plan to the Heads of Government in 1975.[50] The CFC was formally established in 1976 as an autonomous, regional, commercial organization with an authorized share capital of US$40 million subscribed by the member countries of CARICOM.[51] The broad objectives of the CFC are to mobilize, plan, and implement all stages of agricultural production in the region; to mobilize funds, technology, and managerial skills from within and outside the region; and to organize and facilitate bulk purchasing of inputs, marketing of agricultural outputs, and other services related to agricultural production.[52] The CFC is also mandated to be active in the production, processing, storage, transportation, and marketing of food. To carry out these measures, it has been given the powers to make investments; to establish, manage, and operate enterprises; to engage directly in the purchase, processing, transportation, marketing, and distribution of products; to engage in financial operations; and to establish subsidiaries and enter into joint enterprises to achieve any of its objectives.[53]

In effect, the CFC functions as a holding company that can engage in a series of production and marketing operations, either individually or in joint enterprises with the private and public sector, and in cooperation with the CDB, CARDI, CARDATS, and other regional agencies. The CFC is designed to be the principal implementing agency of the subsectoral projects in the Regional Food Plan by serving as a commercially oriented, publicly owned agribusiness investment and development company. As such, it will undertake activities currently carried out by few companies in the private sector (most of which are subsidiaries of multinationals) in a way that is compatible with the economic and social development goals of the member countries.[54] It is also envisaged that the CFC will attract and channel funding from donor agencies into regional projects aimed at restructuring agricultural production.

Although formally established in 1976, the CFC did not begin operation until 1980. To assist it in starting up, a UNDP/CDB support project was initiated in 1978 with funding amounting to US$2.0 million. This project provided aid for the preparation of projects under the Regional Food Plan, technical assistance for on-going projects supporting research and development relating to improved technology for small farmers, and start-up support for the CFC.[55] The priorities it established for the first years of operation were as follows: (1) an emphasis on the development of a regional marketing system for agricultural inputs and outputs, as well as on bulk purchasing and packaging for the LDCs; (2) efforts to reduce wastage in food processing resulting from seasonal blockages, to widen the range of products and improve quality control, and to reduce the degree of underutilization of processing capacity resulting from lack of inputs and plant inflexibility; and (3) preparation of production projects, some thirty of which are presently being studied and four of which are ready for investment.

In 1982 the Caribbean Food Corporation established a trading subsidiary, the Caribbean Agricultural Trading Corporation (CATCO). This latter corporation is a joint venture between the CFC and a major private food company in the region, Grace Kennedy, which owns 49 percent of the company and has a three-year management contract that gives it responsibility for the management of CATCO. The chairman of Grace Kennedy is also the chairman of CATCO. CATCO is seen as a means to approach the problem of agricultural marketing in a region where public marketing corporations have failed in the past. It also represents an attempt to take advantage of the experience of the private sector in importing and distributing food products in the region as well as in food processing. It can be seen as a move away from political concerns toward commercial concerns in the area of food marketing.

The model of CATCO as it has emerged diverges somewhat from the original conception of the CFC. It aims to create a system of production and marketing at the regional level by securing intra- and extraregional markets for particular commodities in specific markets. This system reflects an emphasis on the marketing rather than the production side of agriculture, and points to greater reliance on the large farmer than on the small farmer of the region. CATCO is also trying to increase the use of agricultural inputs such as fertilizers and pesticides with emphasis on the LDCs.

The principal undertakings of CATCO include (1) establishment of a regional agricultural marketing system with representatives in each territory; (2) the development of an efficient and integrated transport and handling system; (3) the identification of intra- and extraregional markets; and (4) the creation of mechanisms for collaboration with other regional institutions, governments, and the private sector.

The manner in which CATCO operates will eventually touch on a number of broader integration issues in the region. The early emphasis on marketing may turn attention away from problems on the production side, and the need to supply specific amounts of particular products for intra- and extraregional markets may reduce benefits for the smaller farmers in the LDCs. The joint venture between the CFC and private enterprise is also likely to influence the relationship between the commercial and political aspects of integration.

In carrying out its mandate, the CFC will have to face a number of issues related to its ambitious objectives and broad powers. The first issue is whether the CFC will adopt an "investment" approach or an "operating" approach. In its early years, its thrust will probably reflect the former option, with the CFC taking a minority position in joint projects rather than a majority position entailing management responsibility. Scarce management resources and the desire for private-sector support and donor-agency appeal are likely to favor the "investment" approach.[56]

A second issue is the relationship between the public and private sector. It is hoped that the CFC can bridge the gap between business and government in the region, and enlist technical, managerial, and financial support from the private sector. In accomplishing these objectives, the CFC is committed to functioning on a "commercial" (i.e., self-financing) basis. A third issue is the conflict between the commitment to operate on a commercial basis and the commitment to take direct action to improve agricultural production in the LDCs. Resolution of this conflict will require that a delicate balance be found between "commercial" projects and "development" projects.

A fourth issue is the degree of overlap and complementarity between the CFC and other regional institutions—an issue that will require cooperation between the CFC and the CDB in the development of agro-industrial projects; between the CFC and the CDB in initiating studies and investing, lending, and coordinating funds from donor agencies; between the CFC and the CARICOM Secretariat in responding to specific needs of the Regional Food and Nutrition Strategy; and between the CFC and CARDI in providing technical assistance for various projects. Ideally, these institutions should be mutually supporting.

A fifth issue derives from the relationship between the activities of the CFC and the national efforts of the member governments in the agricultural sector. The CFC is empowered to operate within the territory of any of the member countries, and its mandate to carry out regional projects is defined broadly to include projects in or involving more than one territory, projects involving one member territory and one regional agency, and projects in one territory whose products will be traded within the region. Care must be taken to ensure coordination and complementarity between regional activities and those of the national governments.

These issues must be resolved as the activities of the CFC progress beyond the current beginning stage. The fact that they exist as real issues is indicative of the extensive powers given to the CFC as a positive measure designed to bring about the transformation of regional agriculture. When considered in conjunction with the broad scope of the Regional Food and Nutrition Strategy, the extensive mandate of the implementing capacity of the Caribbean Food Corporation gives the Caribbean the most far-reaching and ambitious program for agricultural development to be found among integration groupings of developing countries. The measures to be taken under the Regional Food and Nutrition Strategy are still in the preliminary stage of adoption, and it will be a number of years before any judgment can be made as to their potential success. Nonetheless, they reflect a serious attempt to come to grips with the problems of agricultural underdevelopment in the Caribbean.

Conclusions

CARICOM has initiated an ambitious plan for regional programming in the agricultural sector that represents the culmination of an evolution of policy from a modified free trade regime toward direct action to bring about agricultural development. As with most integration schemes among developing countries, CARIFTA's early agricultural efforts consisted of a limited free trade policy as an adjunct to *laissez-faire* integration policies designed to bring about industrial import substitution on a regional scale. When this policy, embodied in the Agricultural Marketing Protocol, failed to provide benefits to the LDCs of the region in compensation for their relative losses in the increased regional trade in manufactured products, it was modified by the addition of the Guaranteed Market Scheme.

The reasoning behind this change was faulty in two aspects. First, it was wrong to think that the LDCs would be satisfied with agricultural gains as a compensation for not participating in industrial gains from integration; second, it was wrong to believe that agricultural production would respond easily to increased market incentives. The failure of the AMP and GMS drew attention to the root causes of agricultural underdevelopment in the region and led to an increasingly *dirigiste* approach to integration in this sector, with the CDB taking a more active role in identifying and initiating the financing of agricultural projects, and with CARDI and CARDATS intervening directly in the production activity of small farmers. With the elaboration of the Regional Food and Nutrition Strategy and the entry into operation of the Caribbean Food Corporation, CARICOM has taken the first steps toward regional planning through sectoral programming.

In short, regional integration policy in the agricultural sector has moved toward the creation of a policy that responds to the needs of integration for development, whereas the broader integration movement has failed to advance beyond the limited customs union negotiated in 1973. This situation provides the basis for significant insights into the process of regional integration among developing countries and into the role of agriculture in that process.

Notes

1. This section is based on a revised version of W. Andrew Axline, "Basic Needs and Integration: Regional Food and Nutrition Policy in the Commonwealth Caribbean" (Paper presented at the annual meeting of the Caribbean Studies Association, St. Thomas, Virgin Islands, May 1981). See also W. Andrew Axline, "Agricultural Cooperation in CARICOM," in Anthony Payne and Paul Sutton, eds., *Dependency Under Challenge: The Political Economy of the Commonwealth Caribbean* (Manchester, England: University of Manchester Press, 1984), pp. 152–173.

2. These commodities are as follows: carrots, peanuts, tomatoes, red kidney beans, black pepper, sweet pepper, garlic, onions, potatoes, sweet potatoes, string beans, cinnamon, cloves, cabbage, plantains, pork and pork products, poultry meat, eggs, okra, fresh oranges, pineapples, and pigeon peas.

3. Prem Arjoon, "Agricultural Integration in CARIFTA: A Unique Experiment," *Guyana Graphic* (September 13–14, 1970).

4. Commonwealth Caribbean Regional Secretariat (CCRS), *CARIFTA and the New Caribbean* (Georgetown, Guyana: CCRS, 1971), pp. 33–34.

5. George E. Buckmire, "Rationalization as an Instrument for Development of Caribbean Agriculture," *Proceedings of the Eighth West Indian Agricultural Economics Conference* (St. Augustine, Trinidad: University of the West Indies [UWI], 1973), p. 12. See also J. M. Mayers, "Some Aspects of Rationalization and Livestock Development in the Commonwealth Caribbean," *Proceedings of the Seventh West Indian Agricultural Economics Conference* (St. Augustine, Trinidad: UWI, 1973), pp. 71–77.

6. Caribbean Common Market, *Treaty Establishing the Caribbean Community*, Annex, Article 49 (1973).

7. B. Persaud, "The Agricultural Marketing Protocol of CARIFTA and the Economic Integration of Agriculture," *Proceedings of the Fourth West Indian Agricultural Economics Conference* (St. Augustine, Trinidad: UWI, 1969), p. 107.

8. Louis L. Smith, *Critical Evaluation of the Performance of the ECCM Countries Under the Agricultural Marketing Protocol (AMP) and the Guaranteed Market Scheme (GMS)*, ECLA/POS74/16 (Port of Spain, Trinidad: Economic Commission for Latin America [ECLA], 1974), p. 2. The CARICOM Treaty contains several articles directly relating to the agricultural sector, the most pertinent of which are Articles 25 and 26 relating to government aids to intraregional trade in agricultural products; Article 48 and its related schedules, VII (Marketing Arrangements for Unrefined Cane Sugar), VIII (AMP), and IX (Marketing Arrangements for Oils and Fats); and Article 49 dealing with rationalization of agricultural production.

9. Buckmire, "Rationalization as an Instrument," p. 9.

10. Smith, *Critical Evaluation*, pp. 1–2.

11. Ibid., p. 2. See also Winston J. Phillips, "Towards a Common Agricultural Policy for the Caribbean Community" (Paper prepared for the Caribbean Community Secretariat/UNDP Multi-Sectoral Regional Planning Project Conference on a Common Agricultural Policy for the Caribbean Community, Port of Spain, Trinidad, 1978), pp. 10–11.

12. Smith, *Critical Evaluation*, p. 3. The commodities selected were peanuts, tomatoes, onions, cabbages, potatoes, sweet potatoes, and carrots.

13. Phillips, "Towards a Common Agricultural Policy," pp. 11–12.

14. Smith, *Critical Evaluation*, p. 3; Phillips, "Towards a Common Agricultural Policy," p. 12.

15. Phillips, "Towards a Common Agricultural Policy," p. 14.

16. Ibid., p. 15; Persaud, "Agricultural Marketing Protocol," pp. 108–109; CARICOM/ECLA, *Study of the Payments Arrangements for AMP Trade* (Port-of-Spain [POS], Trinidad: ECLA/POS, n.d.), pp. 2–12; Gloria Francis, *Food Crop Production in Barbados and Its Response to CARIFTA/CARICOM and the AMP*, Occasional Paper no. 2 (Cave Hill, Barbados: UWI, Institute of Social and Economic Research [Eastern Caribbean branch], 1975), pp. 36–46.

17. The World Bank recognized these structural obstacles in its 1975 Regional Study of the Caribbean: "The AMP as well as the GMS are likely to be more successful in encouraging output and exports of the LDCs if

they were part of active efforts to deal with the structural, basic factors inhibiting production." See "Agriculture," in *IBRD Caribbean Regional Study*, Vol. 3, Report no. 566A (Washington, D.C.: IBRD, 1975), p. 16. See also George E. Buckmire, "Agriculture in the CARIFTA Economic Integration Movement," document submitted to the Seminar on Agricultural Integration (Washington, D.C.: Inter-American Development Bank, 1971), pp. 6–17.

18. George L. Beckford, *Persistent Poverty: Underdevelopment in Plantation Economies of the Third World* (New York: Oxford University Press, 1972).

19. E.R. St. J. Cumberbatch, "Man and the Land in the Caribbean" (Paper prepared for an International Rural Development Conference, Montreal, McDonald College, 1976); S. Norman Girwar, "The Role and Future of Sugar in the Commonwealth Caribbean in the Light of Britain's Entry into the EEC," *Proceedings of the Seventh West Indian Agricultural Economics Conference* (St. Augustine, Trinidad: UWI, 1973), pp. 24–26.

20. United Nations/ECLA, *Report of the Caribbean Regional Workshop on Integrated Rural Development*, E/CN.12/846 (Kingston, Jamaica: UN, 1969), p. 20; E.R. St. J. Cumberbatch, "Prospects for Caribbean Agriculture" (Paper prepared for the Second Caribbean Seminar on Scientific and Technological Planning, St. Augustine, Trinidad, 1976), p. iii; Curtis E. McIntosh and Michael Lim Choy, *The Performance of Selected Agricultural Marketing Agencies*, Occasional Series no. 16 (St. Augustine, Trinidad: UWI, Department of Agricultural Economics and Farm Management, 1975), pp. 2–4.

21. Louis A. Campbell, "Strategy for Maximising Self-Sufficiency in Food in the Region," *Proceedings of the Tenth West Indies Agricultural Economics Conference* (St. Augustine, Trinidad: UWI, 1975), pp. 54–63; F. Wyke, "Linkages Between Agriculture and Industry in the Commonwealth Caribbean," *Proceedings of the Fourth West Indian Agricultural Economics Conference* (St. Augustine, Trinidad: UWI, 1969), p. 39; B. Persaud and L. Persaud, "The Impact of Agricultural Diversification Policies in Barbados in the Post-War Period," *Selected Papers for the Third West Indian Agricultural Economics Conference* (St. Augustine, Trinidad: UWI, 1968), pp. 353–364; George E. Beckford, "Land Reform for the Betterment of Caribbean Peoples," *Proceedings of the Seventh West Indian Agricultural Economics Conference* (St. Augustine, Trinidad: UWI, 1972), pp. 25–39; Vincent R. McDonald, "The Role of Land Reform in Economic Development Among Caribbean Countries," photocopy (n.d.), 26 pp.; George E. Buckmire, "Land Use and Agricultural Development in the Commonwealth Caribbean," *Proceedings of the Seventh West Indian Agricultural Economics Conference* (St. Augustine, Trinidad: UWI, 1972), pp. 40–42.

22. K. A. Leslie, "Contribution of Agriculture to Economic Development: A Case Study of the West Indies—1950–1963," *Proceedings of the First West Indian Agricultural Economics Conference* (St. Augustine, Trinidad: UWI, 1967), p. 72.

23. W. Andrew Axline, *Caribbean Integration: The Politics of Integration* (London: Frances Pinter, and New York: Nichols Publishing Co., 1979); Caribbean Development Bank, *Annual Report 1976*; CARICOM Secretariat,

"Towards the Development of the Agricultural Sector of the Caribbean Community: The Regional Food Plan and the Regional Food and Nutrition Strategy," *CARICOM Bulletin,* no. 3 (1982):11.

24. Caribbean Development Bank, *Annual Report 1983,* p. 11. The CDB policies on regional agriculture are spelled out in Caribbean Development Bank, "Agriculture" (Sector policy paper, Barbados, 1961).

25. Caribbean Development Bank, *Annual Report 1980,* p. 9. In 1981, the CDB adopted a new system of classification in which food processing and nutrition are placed under the headings of manufacturing and social and personal services respectively, thus making comparison with earlier periods impossible.

26. Ibid., p. 54.

27. Development Management Consultants, *An Evaluation of the Farm Improvement Credit Scheme* (Bridgetown, Barbados: Caribbean Development Bank, 1980). Among the DFCs, it is only in St. Lucia and in Belize that the administration of the FIC scheme seems to have been well carried out.

28. Caribbean Development Bank, *Annual Report 1983,* p. 54.

29. For an extensive survey of the conditions of the small farmer in the Caribbean, see Caribbean Development Bank (CDB), *Small Farming in the Less Developed Countries of the Commonwealth Caribbean,* Report prepared by Weir's Agricultural Services, Jamaica (Barbados: CDB, 1980). See also Donald R. Fiester, William Baucom, Alphose Chable, and Clarence Zuvekas, Jr., *Agricultural Development in the Eastern Caribbean: A Survey* (Washington, D.C.: USAID, 1978).

30. *Sunday Guardian* (Trinidad), 21 November 1976, p. 1.

31. CARDI Agricultural Information Services, "Caribbean Agricultural Research and Development Institute," pamphlet (Bridgetown, Barbados, 1980). On R&D in Caribbean agriculture, see Carleton G. Davis, "Agricultural Research and Agricultural Development in Small Plantation Economies: The Case of the West Indies," *Social and Economic Studies* 24 (March 1975):117–149. See also L. B. Coke and P. I. Gomes, "Critical Analysis of Agricultural Research and Development Institutions and Their Activities," *Social and Economic Studies* 28 (March 1979):97–138.

32. Phillips, "Towards a Common Agricultural Policy," p. 38.

33. Hayden Blades, "The Regional Food Plan," *CARICOM Bulletin* 1 (August 1978):20.

34. Eric Williams, "The Caribbean Food Crisis" (Address to the Caribbean Veterinary Association, Office of the Prime Minister, Port of Spain, Trinidad, August 12, 1974).

35. Caribbean Community Secretariat, *CARICOM Feeds Itself: Basic Answers to the Questions Most Often Asked About the Regional Food Plan* (Georgetown, Guyana: CARICOM Secretariat, 1977), p. 23.

36. International Bank for Reconstruction and Development (IBRD), *Regional Agricultural Development and Food Production in the Caribbean,* Report no. 2064-CRB (Washington, D.C.: IBRD, 1978), pp. 5–6; Blades, "The Regional Food Plan," p. 21.

37. Caribbean Community Secretariat, *CARICOM Feeds Itself: Basic Answers*, pp. 8–10.

38. Blades, "The Regional Food Plan," p. 23.

39. "The Regional Food Plan: A Progress Report," *CARICOM Perspective* 2 (May 1980):3–6; IBRD, *Regional Agricultural Development and Food Production in the Caribbean*, pp. 12–22.

40. "The Regional Food Plan: A Progress Report," p. 6.

41. CARICOM Secretariat, Inter-Sectoral Committee, *CARICOM Feeds Itself: A Regional Food and Nutrition Strategy—A Strategy for the 80s*, working document prepared for the Technical Group Meeting on the Regional Food and Nutrition Strategy, Kingston, Jamaica, November 24–28, 1980 (Georgetown, Guyana: CARICOM Secretariat, 1980). A broader discussion of efforts to improve the production side of agriculture are found in CARICOM Secretariat, *The Caribbean Community in the 1980s* (Georgetown, Guyana: CARICOM Secretariat, 1982), pp. 44–49.

42. CARICOM Secretariat, *CARICOM Feeds Itself: A Regional Food and Nutrition Strategy*, Preface, p. vii.

43. Ibid., ch. 1, p. 7.

44. Ibid., ch. 3, p. 13.

45. Ibid., ch. 3, p. 1.

46. Caribbean Food and Nutrition Institute (CFNI), *The Caribbean Food Plan: An Economic Framework* (Mona, Jamaica: CFNI, 1978), cited in CARICOM Secretariat, *CARICOM Feeds Itself: A Regional Food and Nutrition Strategy*, ch. 3, p. 2.

47. CARICOM Secretariat, *CARICOM Feeds Itself*, ch. 3, p. 3.

48. Ibid., ch. 3, pp. 3–9.

49. The elaborate proposed organizational structure is described in ibid., ch. 11.

50. Government of Jamaica, Ministry of Agriculture, *Caribbean Food Corporation*, Ministry Paper no. 46 (Kingston, Jamaica: Government Printery, 1976), p. 2.

51. IBRD, *Regional Agricultural Development and Food Production in the Caribbean*, p. 9.

52. Caribbean Community Secretariat, *CARICOM Feeds Itself: Basic Answers*, p. 17.

53. Caribbean Food Corporation, *Agreement Establishing the Caribbean Food Corporation*, Articles 3 and 5 (August 18, 1974).

54. Clyde C. Applewhite, *The Caribbean Food Corporation: Concept and Functions* (Barbados: CDB, 1979), pp. 3, 7. See also Caribbean Food Corporation, *Profile of the Caribbean Food Corporation (CFC)* (Port-of-Spain, Trinidad: CFC, 1981).

55. Applewhite, *The Caribbean Food Corporation*, pp. 13–14.

56. Ibid., p. 19.

6
Epilogue: Basic Needs and Collective Self-Reliance

The history of Caribbean integration exemplifies the general evolution of the politics of regional integration among developing countries. This is evident in the overall Caribbean integration movement as well as in the specific policy area of agriculture. From the phased freeing of trade approach to integration adopted at the 1967 Georgetown Conference and reflected in the CARIFTA Agreement, Caribbean integration has moved toward a more positive type of regional cooperation; along the way, it has adopted policies to redress imbalances among member countries and has proposed policies to reduce dependence. Both sets of policies have been debated with respect to the differences among the more and less developed countries of the region, with an emphasis on the issue of distribution of gains.

Although the "deepening" of Caribbean integration that occurred with the creation of CARICOM reflected a response to the development needs of the region, the integration movement continued to follow the *laissez-faire* approach that marked its beginnings. Even the Draft Agreement on Foreign Investment and Development of Technology, which was rejected, had been strongly influenced by this generally liberal thrust of integration. Whereas the overall integration movement remains directed toward this market approach, there are indications that within the agricultural sector regional policies reflect a shift toward integration of production.

In the overall process of regional integration, CARICOM has reached a point of stagnation, having "deepened" the integration process with the adoption of an external tariff and additional distributive measures in 1973 and having failed to adopt a regime to control foreign investment and transfer of technology in 1974. CARICOM has successfully adopted a series of measures to create net gains for the region and measures to distribute the gains equitably, but it has failed to satisfy the third requirement of adopting measures to reduce the negative effects of dependency. After early years of regional trade expansion, intraregional trade is now declining as a portion of total trade. The Caribbean Investment Corporation, which was seen as the major concession to the LDCs in exchange for their support for the Common External Tariff, is now defunct. And the early *laissez faire* measures designed to increase agricultural trade—the Agricultural Marketing Protocol and the Guaranteed Market Scheme—have been abandoned.

With respect to the Regional Food and Nutrition Strategy, however, the implementation of subsectoral projects by the CFC provides the potential of achieving all three objectives (expansion of benefits, equitable distribution of benefits, and reduction of dependence) within the agricultural sector. This evolution in CARICOM toward more intensive integration on a less extensive scale (limited to a single sector) is illustrative of the response of regional integration as it evolves to meet the needs and conditions of underdeveloped countries. Indeed, this type of cooperation has moved so far away from traditional customs union theory that it would be misleading, perhaps, to refer to it as integration. More correctly, it is a form of regional cooperation among developing countries (RCDC) that is sometimes referred to as *collective self-reliance*—a term that describes the common action taken among developing countries to restructure their relationship with third countries, particularly the metropole, as a part of the effort being made to bring about a more self-sufficient process of development. Within the agricultural sector, CARICOM's policies clearly reflect the evolution of Caribbean integration in this direction. The Oils and Fats Agreement and the Rice Agreements provided the basis for the Agricultural Marketing Protocol; all of these policies are aimed at contributing to agricultural development through market solutions—namely, solutions entailing the orderly organization of regional markets in certain food products, along with a region-wide system of protection. The modification of the AMP through the creation of the Guaranteed Market Scheme reflected the recognition that some intervention was required to ensure that the LDCs would benefit from these agricultural provisions. Similarly, the special agricultural credit schemes of the Caribbean Development Bank, as well as the FIC and APC programs, provided needed facilities on the production side.

With the establishment of CARDI and CARDATS, regional agricultural policy moved toward more direct action in promoting production by direct intervention at the farm level. Moreover, the creation of the Caribbean Food Corporation provided a regional institution endowed with extensive powers to undertake direct action in the production and marketing of agricultural inputs and commodities.

Finally, the elaboration of the Regional Food and Nutrition Strategy represented the first step in regional sectoral programming, the central element of an approach to integration based on integration of production. Within the agricultural sector, Caribbean regional policy is beginning to move away from the purely market approach to integration that was adopted in 1967 and has continued to dominate the integration movement. The difficulty in moving toward an integration of production approach in CARICOM might prove to be more easily overcome within the single sector of agricultural policy than it proved to be in the industrial sector.

If CARICOM succeeds in its efforts to move toward regional sectoral programming in agriculture despite the crisis in the overall integration movement, its success will be due partly to the fact that the efforts are limited to a single sector and partly to the fact that agriculture has not been the central focus of political controversy in the region. In this sense, the fact that integration has focused mainly on the industrial sector may contribute to the probability of success in agricultural integration. But before regional sectoral programming can be judged a success or failure in CARICOM, a number of obstacles to its adoption and implementation must be overcome. These obstacles can be seen as a series of contradictions that must be resolved as a basic prerequisite to CARICOM's eventual success.

One contradiction that underlies the whole discussion of regional integration among developing countries is the emphasis on efficiency derived from the confrontation between traditional customs union theory and the development need of increased production even at low levels of efficiency. This issue is of central importance for the region as a whole, but it is also particularly crucial to the matter of allocating production among member countries on the basis of equitable distribution of gains in ways different from those dictated by purely "economic" criteria. Implementation of agricultural policy in CARICOM must be undertaken with due consideration of this contradiction.

First of all, projects in the agricultural sector must reconcile the necessity to employ underutilized and idle regional resources in regional production for local needs, particularly in the LDCs, with the necessity to satisfy reasonable requirements of efficiency. This is a problem for all aspects of integration among developing countries that must satisfy both the "economic" and the "political" requirements of regional policies. In the implementation of CARICOM's agriculture policy, the CFC will have to face this contradiction directly in striking a balance between the "commercial" and the "development" subprojects it undertakes.

Within the region, the terms *commercial* and *development* as used in this context have become code words for *free enterprise* and *state intervention,* respectively, and therefore are highly charged ideologically. The ideological differences within and among the countries of the region potentially pose an obstacle to the realization of the regional objectives. Wide differences exist among the ideological orientations of the governments—orientations that are reflected in the attitudes of these governments toward the role of private enterprise. These ideological differences may be the basis for some disagreement as to the way the CFC should operate in its relationship with the private sector of the region. An indication of these underlying differences can be found in the contrast between the leader of the business community in Barbados who denounced the CFC activities as unwarranted state intervention in the private sector and the editorial in the Guyana *Chronicle* stating that capitalist ideas must not allowed to be entrenched in CFC projects.[1]

The Caribbean Food Corporation was not explicitly designed as a corrective measure—a fact that has caused some consternation among the LDCs. As late as 1977, there was some doubt as to whether the LDCs would go along with a measure that they believed principally benefited the larger territories. The East Caribbean territories were hesitant about participating with Montserrat (and were the last to sign the CARICOM agreement), but by March 1978, all CARICOM countries had paid their initial subscription to the CFC.

In effect, the lack of an explicit distributive element in the CFC reflected concern within the region, particularly on the part of the private sector, that it be operated according to good business principles—that is, with considerations of efficiency prevailing over political principles of equitable distribution of benefits. Within the Caribbean Association of Industry and Commerce, a difference of opinion occurred regarding the CFC; the organization officially denied through its president, Charles Maynard, that the CAIC opposed the plan after one of its members had been quoted as characterizing it as "a monstrous bureaucratic undertaking designed by civil servants for implementation by businessmen."[2] There has been a growing concern on the part of the business community that CARICOM, inspired by the policies of Guyana, would move toward greater state control of economic activity within the region. The business community considered Guyana's External Trade Bureau (ETB) a particularly noxious example of state control and adamantly opposed similar attempts to establish bulk purchasing on a regional level. The same sentiment is reflected in a CAIC resolution adopted by the Board of Directors in 1976:

Whereas the CAIC promoted the organisation as a vehicle for the protection of the concept of private enterprise in the Caribbean as represented by Individual Associations, and Whereas in the Caribbean today there are indications that freedom of expression, freedom to own property, and freedom to own and operate business enterprises in a free market economy within the Rule of Law are being assailed by forces dedicated to the destruction of these rights in the name of social change, and Whereas such ideologies are totally incompatible with the spirit and function of the CAIC, Be it hereby resolved that the CAIC states its firm and unyielding support for the concept of a free man in a free society as the engine to produce the goods and services needed by that society and thus to achieve maximum economic growth within the overall framework of national policies and objectives.[3]

The Caribbean Food Corporation, by virtue of its power to undertake integrated regional planning in the agricultural sector, provides the context in which the contradiction between the need for *dirigiste* measures of integration and the limits of *laissez-faire* ideology becomes apparent. At the same time, the CFC represents the point at which the balance between the technical requirements of economic efficiency and the political requirements of equitable distribution of benefits must be struck. In the future, the aforementioned contradiction will provide the basis for one of the most interesting and important debates of Caribbean integration, given both the major role that the agricultural sector must play in regional development and the central political issues with respect to Third World regional integration that arise in the operation of the CFC.

Another contradiction that underlies integration in general is the requirement for comprehensive decision making and complex administrative institutions needed to carry out ambitious integration policies in a situation in which administrative skills are in short supply. Nowhere is this contradiction more starkly represented than in the complex organizational structure proposed for the Regional Food and Nutrition Strategy, which requires coordination among numerous national and regional agencies. The Regional Food and Nutrition Strategy contains a blueprint for the creation of an institutional structure designed to carry out regional policies, but the ambitious nature of these institutions and the existing shortage of administrative personnel puts into question the feasibility of such a complex structure. The difficulty of the administrative challenge involved becomes even more evident when the degree of coordination required among existing regional institutions is taken into account. The CARICOM Secretariat must play a central role in the formulation of overall regional agricultural strategy. In addition, the Caribbean Development Bank and the Caribbean Food Corporation share responsibility in identifying specific projects, undertaking prefeasibility and feasibility studies, and arranging financing (normally, the CFC alone would be responsible for implementation).

The need for extensive cooperation at the national and regional levels points to the potential contradiction between the policies pursued by the member governments to bring about agricultural development within their territories and the regional policies aimed at rationalizing agriculture on a region-wide basis. This contradiction may operate in two ways. On the one hand, the far-reaching objectives of the Regional Food and Nutrition Strategy may have the effect of encouraging governments to neglect their responsibility for enacting national agricultural policies supportive of the regional measures, thus reducing their likelihood of success. On the other hand, policies to achieve greater self-sufficiency on a national basis may create an obstacle to greater regional self-sufficiency through rationalization. The establishment of the Food and Agriculture Corporation in Trinidad and Tobago, with a mandate similar to that of the CFC, raises the possibility of this kind of conflict. Similarly, the ambitious objectives of the Food and Nutrition Strategy require specific measures that can be taken only by the individual governments (as in the case of land reform)— a policy that is highly charged politically and, in some member countries, likely to be strongly resisted.

It must not be forgotten that the ambitious goals of regional sectoral programming contained in the Food and Nutrition Strategy are still in the early stages, and that they remain to be fully adopted and implemented. Many separate and disparate actions must be coordinated, priorities must be set, and individual political decisions must be made. It is clear that the restructuring of the agricultural sector of the region will require a massive effort directed at all stages in the production and distribution cycle, at both the national and the regional levels.

It appears that agriculture is being accorded a high priority in CARICOM, as evidenced by the comprehensive nature of proposed regional policies put forth by the Secretariat and the large proportion of CDB funds allocated to this sector. This impression was strengthened by the decision of regional officials in September 1980 to leave intact the amount allocated to agricultural projects under the European Development Fund aid when the total amount was cut from an expected US$200 million to $70 or $80 million.

Perhaps the most fundamental question related to Caribbean regional agricultural policy is whether cooperation can proceed in this sector in spite of the continuing stalemate within CARICOM as a whole. Will blocked integration efforts prevent any forward movement on this question, or can solutions be found that will permit this more intensive integration on a less extensive scale? If CARICOM can succeed in the latter action despite the stagnation in the broader integration movement, it will do so specifically because the policies in the agricultural sector contain the elements of (1) increasing regional gains, (2) equitably distributing these gains, and (3) overcoming the constraints of dependency. Success in the agricultural sector may or may not contribute to a renewal of the stalled integration movement; but whatever the outcome, regional policies in this sector provide the most far-reaching example to date of an attempt to satisfy basic needs through collective self-reliance.

Notes

1. The latter incident was reported by the Caribbean News Agency (CANA) wire service on June 8, 1977.

2. *Sunday Advocate* (Barbados), 22 February 1976.

3. Caribbean Association of Industry and Commerce, Inc., *Minutes of the 44th Meeting of the Board of Directors* (Port of Spain, Trinidad, February 6 and 7, 1976).

Abbreviations

AMP	Agricultural Marketing Protocol
APC	Agricultural Production Credit
ASEAN	Association of South East Asian Nations
CACM	Central American Common Market
CAIC	Caribbean Association of Industry and Commerce
CAP	Common Agricultural Policy
CARDATS	Caribbean Agricultural and Rural Development Advisory and Training Service
CARDI	Caribbean Agricultural Research and Development Institute
CARICOM	Caribbean Community and Common Market
CARIFTA	Caribbean Free Trade Association
CATCO	Caribbean Agricultural Trading Corporation
CCC	Caribbean Council of Consumers
CCL	Caribbean Congress of Labour
CDB	Caribbean Development Bank
CEAO	La Communauté économique de l'Afrique de l'Ouest
CET	Common External Tariff
CFC	Caribbean Food Corporation
CIC	Caribbean Investment Corporation
CMEA	Council for Mutual Economic Assistance
DFC	Development Finance Corporation
EAC	East African Community
ECCA	East Caribbean Currency Authority
ECCB	East Caribbean Central Bank
ECCM	East Caribbean Common Market
ECLA	Economic Commission for Latin America
ECOWAS	Economic Community of West African States
EDF	European Development Fund
EEC	European Economic Community

ETB	External Trading Bureau (Guyana)
FAO	Food and Agricultural Organization
FIC	Farm Improvement Credit
GMS	Guaranteed Market Scheme
GROW	Growing and Reaping Our Wealth (Jamaica)
HGC	Heads of Government Conference
IBRD	International Bank for Reconstruction and Development (World Bank)
ICCC	Incorporated Commonwealth Chambers of Industry and Commerce of the Caribbean
IDA	International Development Agency
IDRC	International Development Research Centre (Canada)
IMF	International Monetary Fund
ISC	Inter-Sectoral Committee
ISER	Institute of Social and Economic Research
JCG	Joint Consultative Group
JLP	Jamaica Labour party
LAFTA	Latin American Free Trade Association
LDC	Less Developed Country (within CARICOM)
MDC	More Developed Country (within CARICOM)
ODA	Overseas Development Administration (United Kingdom)
OECD	Organization for Economic Cooperation and Development
OECS	Organisation of Eastern Caribbean States
RCD	Regional Cooperation for Development
RCDC	Regional Cooperation Among Developing Countries
SIECA	Permanent Secretariat of the General Treaty on Central American Economic Integration
UDEAC	L'Union douanière des Etats de l'Afrique centrale
UNDP	United Nations Development Program
USAID	United States Agency for International Development
UWI	University of the West Indies
WISA	West Indies Associated States

Selected Bibliography

Books and Monographs

Adams, John E., 1976. *Environmental and Cultural Factors in the Decline of Agriculture in a Small West Indian Island.* Madison: University of Wisconsin, Center for Latin American Studies (Center Essays, No. 7).

Alexander, Medford, ed., 1975. *Seminar on Agricultural Policy: A Limiting Factor in the Development Process.* Washington, D.C.: Inter-American Development Bank.

Anderson, T., ed., 1974. *Agriculture in the Economy of the Caribbean: A Bibliography.* Madison: University of Wisconsin Land Tenure Center (Publication no. 24).

Axline, W. Andrew, 1979. *Caribbean Integration: The Politics of Regionalism.* London: Frances Pinter; New York: Nichols Publishing.

Aykroyd, W. R., 1967. *Sweet Malefactor: Sugar, Slavery, and Human Society.* London: Heinemann.

Beckford, George L., 1972. *Persistent Poverty: Underdevelopment in Plantation Economies of the Third World.* New York: Oxford University Press.

Beckford, George L., and Witter, Michael, 1980. *Small Garden . . . Bitter Weed.* Morant Bay, Jamaica: Maroon Publishing House.

Brack, D. M., 1964. "Peasant Agriculture in Barbados: A Case Study of a Rural System." Montreal: McGill University (Ph.D. dissertation).

Braithwaite, Edward Kamau, 1974. *Contradictory Omens: Cultural Diversity and Integration in the Caribbean.* Port of Spain, Trinidad: Savacou Publications Ltd. (Monograph no. 1).

Bryden, John M., 1968. *The Contribution of Agriculture to Economic Growth in the Former Federation of the West Indies 1955–65.* St. Augustine, Trinidad: University of the West Indies, Department of Agricultural Economics and Farm Management (Occasional Series no. 3).

Campbell, L. G., and Edwards, David, 1965. *Agriculture in Antigua's Economy: Possibilities and Problems of Adjustment.* Cave Hill, Barbados: Institute of Social and Economic Research (Eastern Caribbean branch).

Clarke, S. St. A., 1962. *The Competitive Position of Jamaica's Agricultural Exports.* Mona, Jamaica: Institute of Social and Economic Research.

Cropper, J., 1974. *Approaches to Developing Integrated Food Crop Production and Processing in Trinidad and Tobago.* St. Augustine, Trinidad: University of the West Indies (Food Crop Policy and Strategy Bulletin no. 1).

Cumberbatch, E.R. St. J., 1977. *Agro-Industrial Science and Technology Needs in Grenada.* Washington, D.C.: Regional Scientific and Technological Development Program (no. 33).

Cumper, G. E., ed., 1960. *The Economy of the West Indies.* Mona, Jamaica: Institute of Social and Economic Research.

Dukhia, J. L., 1975. "Agriculture and Economic Integration with Special Reference to the Caribbean." Reading, England: University of Reading (Ph.D. dissertation).

Floto, E., 1977. *Agrarian Dualism in a Non-Agricultural Economy.* Cambridge, England: University of Cambridge, Centre of Latin American Studies (Working Paper no. 29).

Floyd, B. N., 1977. *Small-Scale Agriculture in Trinidad: A Caribbean Case Study in the Problems of Transforming Rural Societies in the Tropics.* Durham, N.C.: University of Durham, Department of Geography (Occasional Publications, New Series, no. 10).

Francis, Gloria E., 1975. *Food Crop Production in Barbados and Its Response to CARIFTA/CARICOM and the AMP.* Cave Hill, Barbados: UWI, Institute of Social and Economic Research (Occasional Paper no. 2).

Garrido Rojas, Jose, ed., 1977. *La Agricultura en la Integracion latinoamericana.* Santiago: Editorial Universitaria.

Hagelberg, G. B., 1974. *The Caribbean Sugar Industries: Constraints and Opportunities.* New Haven, Conn.: Yale University Antilles Research Program (Occasional Paper no. 3).

Jefferson, Owen, 1972. *The Post-War Economic Development of Jamaica.* Mona, Jamaica: Institute of Social and Economic Research.

Jones, Grant D., 1971. *The Politics of Agricultural Development in Northern British Honduras.* Wake Forest University, Overseas Research Center (Developing Nations Monograph Series 1, no. 4).

Knight, F. W., 1978. *The Caribbean: The Genesis of a Fragmented Nationalism.* London: Oxford University Press.

Lewars, Gladstone, 1977. *Small Farm Financing in Guyana, 1968–1970.* Mona, Jamaica: Institute of Social and Economic Research, University of the West Indies (Programme of Regional Monetary Studies, no. 6).

Marie, J. M., 1980. *Agricultural Diversification in a Small Economy—The Case for Dominica.* Cave Hill, Barbados: Institute of Social and Economic Research (Occasional Paper no. 10).

Marshall, Trevor G., 1974. *A Bibliography of the Commonwealth Peasantry, 1838–1974.* Cave Hill, Barbados: Institute of Social and Economic Research.

May, Jacques M., and McLellan, Donna L., 1972. *The Ecology of Malnutrition in Mexico and Central America.* New York: Hafner Publishing Company (Studies in Medical Geography, vol. 11).

———, 1973. *The Ecology of Malnutrition in the Caribbean.* New York: Hafner Publishing Company (Studies in Medical Geography, vol. 12).

———, 1974. *The Ecology of Malnutrition in Eastern South America.* New York: Hafner Publishing Company (Studies in Medical Geography, vol. 13).

McIntosh, Curtis E., and Lim Choy, Michael, 1975. *The Performance of Selected Agricultural Marketing Agencies.* St. Augustine, Trinidad: University of the West Indies, Department of Agricultural Economics and Farm Management (Occasional Series, no. 16).

Mitchell, James Fitz, 1972. *Land Reform in the Caribbean.* Bridgetown, Barbados: Caribbean Graphic Production, Ltd.

Payne, Anthony, and Sutton, Paul, eds., 1984. *Dependency Under Challenge: The Political Economy of the Commonwealth Caribbean.* Manchester, England: University of Manchester Press.

Rankine, Lloyd B., et al., 1972. *Economic Evaluation of Food Crops Produced on Selected Farms in St. Vincent, 1970–71.* St. Augustine, Trinidad: University of the West Indies, Department of Agricultural Economics and Farm Management (Occasional Series no. 7).

Scrimshaw, Nevin S., and Behar, Moises, 1976. *Nutrition and Agricultural Development: Significance for the Tropics.* New York: Plenum Books.

Shephard, C. Y., 1945. *Peasant Agriculture in the Leeward and Windward Islands.* St. Augustine, Trinidad: UWI, Imperial College of Tropical Agriculture.

Shillingford, John D., 1972. *The Major Agricultural Land Types in Dominica, W. I., and Their Potential for Development.* Ithaca, N.Y.: Cornell University (Cornell International Agricultural Development Monograph no. 36).

Thomas, Clive Y., 1974. *Dependence and Transformation: The Economics of the Transformation to Socialism.* New York: Monthly Review Press.

University of Cambridge and University of London, 1972. *Symposium on Landlord and Peasant in the Caribbean.* Cambridge, England: University of Cambridge, Latin American Institute.

Wells, C. F., et al., 1973. *Jamaica's Food Processing and Packaging Industry.* Mona, Jamaica: CFN.

Williams, Eric, 1964. *Capitalism and Slavery.* London: Andre Deutsch.

Yudelman, Montague, and Howard, Frederic, 1970. *Agricultural Development and Economic Integration in Latin America.* London: Allen & Unwin.

Articles and Papers

Adams, Nassau A., 1968. "An Analysis of Food Consumption and Food Import Trends in Jamaica, 1950–1963." *Social and Economic Studies* 17 (March):1–22.

Alleyne, F., 1972. "Financing Agrarian Reform in the Commonwealth Caribbean." *Proceedings of the Seventh West Indian Agricultural Economics Conference.* St. Augustine, Trinidad: University of the West Indies, pp. 8–14.

——— , 1974. "The Expansion of Tourism and Its Concomitant Unrealised Potential for Agricultural Development in the Barbadian Economy." *Proceedings of the Ninth West Indian Agricultural Economics Conference.* St. Augustine, Trinidad: University of the West Indies, pp. 143–152.

Applewhite, Clyde C., 1979. "The Caribbean Food Corporation: Concept and Functions." Bridgetown, Barbados: mimeograph.

Axline, W. Andrew, 1977. "Underdevelopment, Dependence and Integration: The Politics of Regionalism in the Third World." *International Organization* 31 (Winter):83–105.

———, 1978. "Integration and Development in the Commonwealth Caribbean: The Politics of Regional Negotiations." *International Organization* 32 (Autumn):953–973.

———, 1981. "Latin American Regional Integration: Alternative Perspectives on a Changing Reality." *Latin American Research Review* 6 (Spring).

———, 1984. "Agricultural Cooperation in CARICOM." In Anthony Payne and Paul Sutton, eds., *Dependency Under Challenge: The Political Economy of the Commonwealth Caribbean*. Manchester, England: University of Manchester Press, pp. 152–178.

Axline, W. Andrew, and Mytelka, Lynn K., 1976. "Société multinationale et intégration régionale dans le Groupe andin et dans la Communauté des Caraïbes." *Etudes internationales* 7 (June):163–192.

Baer, Donald, 1976. "Agriculture: A Rediscovered Strategic Sector for Economic Development." *Caribbean Basin Economic Review* 2 (March/April):1–8.

Banfield, R., 1972. "The Role of Agriculture in the Economy of Grenada." *Proceedings of the Seventh West Indian Agricultural Economics Conference.* St. Augustine, Trinidad: University of the West Indies, pp. 133–154.

Barros Charlin, Raymundo, 1977. "El Marco Jurídico de la Integración Agricola." In Jose Garrido Rojas, ed., *La Agricultura en la Integracíon latinoamericana*. Santiago: University of Chile.

Baynes, Ronald A., 1978. "Comments on St. Kitts/Nevis Agricultural Policy and Institutional Arrangements." St. Kitts, Leeward Islands (Paper prepared for the thirteenth Annual Agro-Economics Conference, April).

Beckford, George L., 1965. "Agriculture and Economic Development." *Caribbean Quarterly* 4.

———, 1969. "The Economics of Agricultural Resource Use and Development in Plantation Economies." *Social and Economic Studies* 18 (December):321–347.

———, 1972a. "Institutional Foundations of Resource Underdevelopment in the Caribbean." In Beckford, *Resource Development in the Caribbean*. Montreal: McGill University, Centre for Developing Area Studies, pp. 21–50.

———, 1972b. "Toward an Appropriate Theoretical Framework for Agricultural Development Planning and Policy." In Vincent R. McDonald, ed., *The Caribbean Economies*. New York: MSS Information Corporation, pp. 105–114.

———. 1972c. "Land Reform for the Betterment of Caribbean Peoples." *Proceedings of the Seventh West Indian Agricultural Economics Conference.* St. Augustine, Trinidad: University of the West Indies, pp. 25–39.

———, 1972d. "Peasant Movements and Agrarian Problems in the West Indies." *Caribbean Quarterly* 18 (March):47–58.

————, 1975. "Caribbean Rural Economy." In George L. Beckford, ed., *Caribbean Economy: Dependence and Backwardness*. Mona, Jamaica: Institute of Social and Economic Research, pp. 77–91.

Bergmann, D., 1974. "Le développement agricole des petites Antilles: Nécessités et difficultés." *Revue Tiers-Monde* 58, pp. 363–380.

Best, Lloyd, 1968a. "A Model of Pure Plantation Economy." *Social and Economic Studies* 17 (September):283–326.

————, 1968b. "Outlines of a Model of Pure Plantation Economy." *Selected Papers from the Third West Indian Agricultural Economics Conference*. St. Augustine, Trinidad: University of the West Indies, pp. 288–326.

Blades, Hayden, 1978. "The Regional Food Plan." *CARICOM Bulletin* 1 (August):20–26.

Bourne, Compton, 1972. "Land Reform in a Sparsely Populated Country with an Indigenous Population: The Case of Guyana." *Proceedings of the Seventh West Indian Agricultural Economics Conference*. St. Augustine, Trinidad: University of the West Indies, pp. 73–87.

Braithwaite, Lloyd, 1968. "Social and Political Aspects of Rural Development in the West Indies." *Selected Papers from the Third West Indian Agricultural Economics Conference*. St. Augustine, Trinidad: University of the West Indies, pp. 264–275.

Brewster, Havelock, 1973. "Economic Dependence: A Quantitative Interpretation." *Social and Economic Studies* 22 (March):90–95.

Brierly, John S., 1974. "Small Farming in Grenada, West Indies," *Manitoba Geographical Studies* 4.

Brown, Headly A., 1969. "Import Substitution and West Indian Agriculture: Theoretical Issues." *Proceedings of the Fourth West Indian Agricultural Economics Conference*. St. Augustine, Trinidad: University of the West Indies, pp. 15–24.

————, 1974. "The Impact of the Tourist Industries on the Agricultural Sectors: The Case of Jamaica." *Proceedings of the Ninth West Indian Agricultural Economics Conference*. St. Augustine, Trinidad: University of the West Indies, pp. 129–142.

Bryden, John M., 1974. "The Impact of the Tourist Industries on the Agricultural Sectors: The Competition for Resources and Food Demand Aspects." *Proceedings of the Ninth West Indian Agricultural Economics Conference*. St. Augustine, Trinidad: University of the West Indies, pp. 153–162.

Buckmire, George E., 1972. "Land Use and Agricultural Development in the Commonwealth Caribbean." *Proceedings of the Seventh West Indian Agricultural Economics Conference*. St. Augustine, Trinidad: University of the West Indies, pp. 40–49.

————, 1973. "Rationalization as an Instrument for Development of Caribbean Agriculture." *Proceedings of the Eighth West Indian Agricultural Economics Conference*. St. Augustine, Trinidad: University of the West Indies, pp. 9–23.

Campbell, Lewis G., 1975. "Strategy for Maximising Self-Sufficiency in Food in the Region." *Proceedings of the Tenth West Indies Agricultural Economics*

Conference. St. Augustine, Trinidad: University of the West Indies, pp. 54–65.

Caribbean Agro-Economic Society, 1978a. "Case Study Report on an Integrated Production and Marketing System for the Antigua Agricultural Sector." *Proceedings of the Twelfth West Indies Agricultural Economics Conference.* St. Augustine, Trinidad: University of the West Indies, pp. 29–114.

———, 1978b. "Report on the Discussion of the Regional Food Plan— 27th April, 1977." *Proceedings of the Twelfth West Indies Agricultural Economics Conference.* St. Augustine, Trinidad: University of the West Indies, pp. 237–246.

CARICOM Secretariat, 1980. "The Regional Food Plan: A Progress Report." *CARICOM Perspective* 2 (May):3–6.

———, 1982a. "The Caribbean Regional Food Plan and the Regional Food and Nutrition Strategy: A Select Bibliography." *CARICOM Bulletin* (no. 3):41–43.

———, 1982b. "Towards the Development of the Agricultural Sector of the Caribbean Community: The Regional Food Plan and the Regional Food and Nutrition Strategy," *CARICOM Bulletin* (no. 3):10–18.

———, 1984. "Patterns of Intraregional Trade in the Caribbean Community." *CARICOM Bulletin* (no. 5):10–44.

Carter, Bernard, and Telfer, Irwin, 1975. "The Philosophy and Experience of Maximising Food Supplies in Guyana." *Proceedings of the Tenth West Indies Agricultural Economics Conference.* St. Augustine, Trinidad: University of the West Indies, pp. 79–99.

Clarke, R., 1978. "Processing Technology for the LDCs in the Caribbean." *Proceedings of the Twelfth West Indies Agricultural Economics Conference.* St. Augustine, Trinidad: University of the West Indies, pp. 148–154.

Coke, L. B., 1979. "Critical Analysis of Agricultural Research and Development Institutions and Their Activities." *Social and Economic Studies* 28 (March):97– 138.

Cumberbatch, E.R. St. J., 1976a. "Man and the Land in the Caribbean." Montreal: McDonald College (Paper prepared for an International Rural Development Conference).

———, 1976b. "Prospects for Caribbean Agriculture" (Paper prepared for the Second Caribbean Seminar on Scientific and Technological Planning) St. Augustine, Trinidad: University of the West Indies.

Cumper, G. E., 1968. "Non-economic Factors Influencing Rural Development Planning." *Selected papers from the Third West Indian Agricultural Economics Conference.* St. Augustine, Trinidad: University of the West Indies, pp. 243–251.

David, W., 1969. "A Large Country in CARIFTA: The Case of Guyana." *Proceedings of the Fourth West Indian Agricultural Economics Conference.* St. Augustine, Trinidad: University of the West Indies.

David, Carlton G., 1975. "Agricultural Research and Agricultural Development in Small Plantation Economies." *Social and Economic Studies* 24 (March):117– 152.

Dellimore, J. H., 1979. "Select Technological Issues in Agro-Industry (I)." *Social and Economic Studies* 28 (March):54–96.

Demas, William G., 1970. "The Prospects for Developing Agriculture in the Small Commonwealth Caribbean Territories: The Role of the Small Farmer." *Proceedings of the Fifth West Indian Agricultural Economics Conference*. St. Augustine, Trinidad: University of the West Indies.

Dolly, David, 1975. "Freedom from Hunger Campaign/Action for Development." Londonderry, Dominica: Food and Agricultural Organization Workshop on Rural Transformation in the Contemporary Caribbean.

Farrell, T.M.A., and Nurse, O. M., 1974. "Oil and Agriculture in the Economic Development of Trinidad and Tobago: Competition or Symbiosis?" *Proceedings of the Ninth West Indian Agricultural Economics Conference*. St. Augustine, Trinidad: University of the West Indies, pp. 117–126.

Fiester, Donald R.; Baucom, William; Chable, Alphonse; and Zuvekas, Clarence, Jr., 1978. "Agricultural Development in the Eastern Caribbean: A Survey." Washington, D.C.: USAID.

Finkel, H. J., 1964. "Patterns of Land Tenure in the Leeward and Windward Islands and Their Relevance to Problems of Agricultural Development." *Economic Geography* 40:163–172.

Francis, Gloria E., 1973. "A Note on the Agricultural Marketing Protocol and Vegetable Production in Barbados." *Proceedings of the Eighth West Indian Agricultural Economics Conference*. St. Augustine, Trinidad: University of the West Indies, pp. 84–95.

Freckleton, Marie, 1982. "Some Thoughts on Balance of Payments Policies in the Caribbean Community." *CARICOM Bulletin* (no. 3):19–25.

Furtado, Celso, 1973. "Underdevelopment and Dependence: The Fundamental Connection." Cambridge, England: University of Cambridge, Centre of Latin American Studies (Working Paper no. 17).

Garlow, David C., 1979. "Banks and the Challenge of Increasing Basin Food Production." *Caribbean Basin Economic Survey* 5 (April/May):1–11.

Garrido Rojas, Jose, 1977. "Consideraciones sobre agricultura y la ALALC." In Jose Garrido Rojas, ed., *La Agricultura en la Integración latinoamericana*. Santiago: University of Chile, pp. 21–64.

Girvan, Norman, 1975. "Aspects of the Political Economy of Race in the Caribbean and the Americas: A Preliminary Interpretation." Mona, Jamaica: Institute of Social and Economic Research (Working Paper no. 7).

Girwar, S. Norman, 1973. "The Role and Future of Sugar in the Commonwealth Caribbean in the Light of Britain's Entry into the EEC." *Proceedings of the Seventh West Indian Agricultural Economics Conference*. St. Augustine, Trinidad: University of the West Indies, pp. 24–41.

Graciarena, Jorge, 1979. "The Basic Needs Strategy as an Option: Its Prospects in the Latin American Context." *CEPAL Review* (August).

Gurney, J. M., 1975. "Available Data on the State of Food and Nutrition of the Peoples of the Commonwealth Caribbean." *Proceedings of the Tenth West Indies Agricultural Economics Conference*. St. Augustine, Trinidad: University of the West Indies, pp. 66–75.

Halcrow, M., and Cave, J. M., 1947. "Peasant Agriculture in Barbados." *Bulletin,* New Series, no. 11 (Government of Barbados, Department of Science and Agriculture).

Hill, V. G., and Williams, S. A., 1974. "The Relationship Between the Bauxite Industry and the Agricultural Sector in Jamaica." *Proceedings of the Ninth West Indian Agricultural Economics Conference.* St. Augustine, Trinidad: University of the West Indies, pp. 81–96.

Hills, T. L.; Iton, S.; and Lundgren, J., 1972. "Farm Fragmentation in the Commonwealth Caribbean: Some Preliminary Observations and Analysis." *Proceedings of the Seventh West Indian Agricultural Economics Conference.* St. Augustine, Trinidad: University of the West Indies, pp. 88–102.

Hope, Kemp R., and Kavid Wilfred L., 1974. "Planning for Development in Guyana: The Experience from 1945 to 1973." *InterAmerican Economic Affairs* 27 (Spring):27–46.

Institute of Social and Economic Research, 1965. "Agriculture in Antigua's Economy: Possibilities and Problems of Adjustment." Cave Hill, Barbados: University of the West Indies, Institute of Social and Economic Research.

James, Preston E., 1957. "Man-Land Relations in the Caribbean Area." In *Caribbean Studies: A Symposium.* Seattle and London: University of Washington Press.

Johnson, I. E., and Strachan, M. O., 1974. "Agricultural Development in Jamaica." *Proceedings of the Ninth West Indian Agricultural Economics Conference.* St. Augustine, Trinidad: University of the West Indies, pp. 3–20.

Johnson, I. E.; Strachan, M. O.; and Johnson, J., 1972. "A Review of Land Settlement in Jamaica." *Proceedings of the Seventh West Indian Agricultural Economics Conference.* St. Augustine, Trinidad: University of the West Indies, pp. 110–132.

Leslie, K. A., 1967. "Contribution of Agriculture to Economic Development: A Case Study of the West Indies—1950–1963." *Proceedings of the First West Indian Agricultural Economics Conference.* St. Augustine, Trinidad: University of the West Indies, pp. 71–77.

Leslie, K. A., and Rankine, L. B., 1975. "Food Supplies in the Commonwealth Caribbean: The Case of Jamaica." *Proceedings of the Tenth West Indies Agricultural Economics Conference.* St. Augustine, Trinidad: University of the West Indies, pp. 23–37.

Lewis, W. Arthur, 1972. "The Caribbean Development Bank." *Proceedings of the Seventh West Indian Agricultural Economics Conference.* St. Augustine, Trinidad: University of the West Indies, pp. 3–7.

Mamalakis, Markos J., 1969. "The Theory of Sectoral Clashes." *Latin American Research Review* 4 (Fall):9–46.

Mark, R., 1972. "A Case of Land Reform in Grenada." *Proceedings of the Seventh West Indian Agricultural Economics Conference.* St. Augustine, Trinidad: University of the West Indies, pp. 155–158.

Marshall, Woodville K., 1968. "Notes on Peasant Development in the West Indies Since 1838." *Selected Papers from the Third West Indian Agricultural*

Economics Conference. St. Augustine, Trinidad: University of the West Indies, pp. 252–263.

—————, 1972. "Peasant Movements and Agrarian Problems in the West Indies: Aspects of the Development of the Peasantry." *Caribbean Quarterly* 18 (March):30–46.

Mayers, John M., 1973. "Some Aspects of Rationalization in the Commonwealth Caribbean." *Proceedings of the Seventh West Indian Agricultural Economics Conference.* St. Augustine, Trinidad: University of the West Indies, pp. 71–77.

—————, 1981. "Towards a Regional Food and Nutrition Strategy." *Bulletin of Eastern Caribbean Affairs* 7 (no. 2):5–11.

McDonald, V., 1973. "Innovation: The Basis for a Programme of Rationalization of Caribbean Agriculture." *Proceedings of the Eighth West Indian Agricultural Economics Conference.* St. Augustine, Trinidad: University of the West Indies, pp. 95–106.

McDonald, Vincent R., n.d. "The Role of Land Reform in Economic Development Among Caribbean Countries." 26 pp. (photocopy).

McMorris, C. S., 1957. "Small Farm Financing in Jamaica." *Social and Economic Studies* 6, no. 3 (supplements).

Medina, Hugo, 1975. "La Integracíon Agricola en la Asociacíon Latinoamericana de Libro Comercio y sus perspectivas." Rome: Paper presented at FAO Seminar on Agriculture in Regional Integration.

Mintz, Sidney W., 1955. "The Jamaican Internal Marketing Patterns: Some Notes and Hypotheses." *Social and Economic Studies* 4 (March).

—————, 1965. "The Question of Caribbean Peasantries: A Comment." *Caribbean Studies* 1 (no. 3):32–34.

—————, 1970. "The Origins of the Jamaican Internal Marketing System." In Sidney Mintz and Douglas Hall, eds., *Papers in Caribbean Anthropology.* New Haven, Conn.: Yale University Press.

—————, 1977. "Was the Plantation Slave a Proletarian?" Binghamton: State University of New York, Braudel Center (Working Paper).

Mitchell, James Fitz, 1972. "The CARIFTA Marketing Protocol: Its Creation and Maintenance." *Tropical Science* 14 (no. 1).

Momsen, Janet D., 1972a. "Land Tenure as a Barrier to Agricultural Innovation: The Case of St. Lucia." *Proceedings of the Seventh West Indian Agricultural Economics Conference.* St. Augustine, Trinidad: University of the West Indies, pp. 103–109.

—————, 1972b. "Report on Vegetable Production and the Tourist Industry in St. Lucia." Calgary, Alberta: University of Calgary Press (mimeo).

—————, 1973. "Report on Vegetable Production and the Tourist Industry in Montserrat." Calgary, Alberta: University of Calgary Press (mimeo).

Newhouse, P., and Alcantara, J., 1969. "Import Substitution in Agriculture: A Case Study of Trinidad and Tobago." *Proceedings of the Fourth West Indian Agricultural Economics Conference.* St. Augustine, Trinidad: University of the West Indies, pp. 26–37.

O'Brien, Hamid, 1974. "The Competition for Resources (Especially Labour and Land) Between the Oil Industry and Agriculture in Trinidad and

Tobago." *Proceedings of the Ninth West Indian Agricultural Economics Conference.* St. Augustine, Trinidad: University of the West Indies, pp. 195–210.

Oteiza, Enrique, 1977. "Collective Self-Reliance Among Developing Countries." In Khadija Haq, ed., *Equality of Opportunity Within and Among Developing Countries.* New York: Praeger Publishers, pp. 81–87.

Otterbein, K. F., 1964. "A Comparison of the Land Tenure Systems of the Bahamas, Jamaica, and Barbados." *International Archives of Ethnography* 50:31–42.

Persaud, B., 1969a. "Agricultural Diversification in the Commonwealth Caribbean: Some Basic Issues." *Proceedings of the Fourth West Indian Agricultural Economics Conference.* St. Augustine, Trinidad: University of the West Indies, pp. 3–7.

———, 1969b. "The Agricultural Marketing Protocol of CARIFTA and the Economic Integration of Agriculture." *Proceedings of the Fourth West Indian Agricultural Economics Conference.* St. Augustine, Trinidad: University of the West Indies, pp. 107–111.

Persaud, B., and Persaud, L., 1968. "The Impact of Agricultural Diversification Policies in Barbados in the Post-War Period." *Selected Papers from the Third West Indian Agricultural Economics Conference.* St. Augustine, Trinidad: University of the West Indies, pp. 353–364.

Phillips, J. W., and Dukhia, J. L., 1974. "The Competition for Resources (Especially Land and Labour) Between Extractive Industries and Agriculture: The Case of Guyana's Bauxite Industry." *Proceedings of the Ninth West Indian Agricultural Economics Conference.* St. Augustine, Trinidad: University of the West Indies, pp. 99–114.

Pilgrim, E. C., 1969. "The Role and Structure of Agriculture in Barbados and the Agricultural Development Programme." *Proceedings of the Fourth West Indian Agricultural Economics Conference.* St. Augustine, Trinidad: University of the West Indies, pp. 55–66.

———, 1970. "The Role and Structure of Agriculture in Barbados and the Agricultural Development Programme." *Bulletin,* No. 1 (Government of Barbados, Ministry of Agriculture).

Rajbansee, J., 1973. "Politico-Administrative Aspects of Agricultural Development: A Caribbean Perspective." Indian Institute of Public Administration.

Richardson, Bonham C., 1972a. "The Agricultural Dilemma of the Post-Plantation Caribbean." *Inter-American Economic Affairs* 26 (Summer):59–70.

———, 1972b. "Guyana's 'Green Revolution': Social and Ecological Problems in the Agricultural Development Programme." *Caribbean Quarterly* 18 (March):14–23.

Roache, K. L., 1976. "Prospects for Agricultural Growth in the Commonwealth Caribbean for the Next Ten Years." In Edith Hodgkinson, ed., *Development Prospects and Options in the Commonwealth Caribbean.* London: Overseas Development Institute.

Ruiz Iriarte, Jorge, 1975. "Planteamientos para el Seminario de la FAO sobre los Problemas Agricolas de los Planes de Integracíon Regional." Rome: Paper presented at the FAO Seminar on Agriculture in Regional Integration.

Sammy, G., 1974. "The Scope for the Development of Food Processing." *Proceedings of the Ninth West Indian Agricultural Economics Conference.* St. Augustine, Trinidad: University of the West Indies, pp. 61–68.

Shillingford, J. D., and Blades, H. W., 1975. "Prospective Demand for Food in the Commonwealth Caribbean." *Proceedings of the Tenth West Indies Agricultural Economics Conference.* St. Augustine, Trinidad: University of the West Indies, pp. 40–53.

Stone, Carl, 1974. "Political Aspects of Post-War Agricultural Policies in Jamaica (1945–1970)." *Social and Economic Studies* 23 (June):145–175.

Tai, E. A., 1978. "Crop Production for Food in Antigua." *Proceedings of the Twelfth West Indies Agricultural Economics Conference.* St. Augustine, Trinidad: University of the West Indies, pp. 123–129.

United Nations, Economic Commission for Latin America and Food and Agricultural Organization, 1975. "The Agricultural Sector in the Economic Integration Systems of Latin America." Rome: Paper presented at the FAO Seminar on Agriculture in Regional Integration.

Vaitsos, Constantine, 1978. "The Attitudes and Role of Transnational Enterprises in Economic Integration Processes Among the LDCs." *Millenium—Journal of International Studies* 6 (Winter 1977-1978):251–269.

Valencia Astorga, Manuel, and Venegas Bahas, Haroldo, 1977. "Intercambio comercial de productos agropecuarios en ALALC y Pacto andino." In Jose Garrido Rojas, ed., *La Agricultura en la Integración latinoamericana.* Santiago: University of Chile, pp. 65–92.

Vining, James W., 1975. "The Rice Economy of Government Settlement Schemes in Guyana." *Inter-American Economic Affairs* 29 (Summer):3–20.

Weber, Adolf, 1977. "Agriculture and Agricultural Policy in Regional Integration Schemes of Developing Countries." Kiel, Germany: Universität Kiel, Lehrsthul fur Agrarpolitik (Diskussionsbeitrage Nr. 29).

Weber, Adolf, and Hartmann, T., 1976. "A Comparative Study of Economic Integration with Special Reference to Agricultural Policy in the East African Community." *Zeitschrift für Auslandische Landwirtschaft* 15:110–127.

Whitehead, Judy A., 1979. "Select Technological Issues in Agro-Industry (II)." *Social and Economic Studies* 28 (March):139–188.

Wyke, F., 1969. "Linkages Between Agriculture and Industry in the Commonwealth Caribbean." *Proceedings of the Fourth West Indian Agricultural Economics Conference.* St. Augustine, Trinidad: University of the West Indies.

Yankey, J. B., 1974. "The Experience of Agriculture and the Rural Sector in Economic Development (with Special Reference to Dominica)." *Proceedings of the Ninth West Indian Agricultural Economics Conference.* St. Augustine, Trinidad: University of the West Indies, pp. 23–29.

Yankey, J. B., and Watty, W.R.F., 1969. "A Small Agricultural Economy in CARIFTA: The Case of Dominica." *Proceedings of the Fourth West Indian*

Agricultural Economics Conference. St. Augustine, Trinidad: University of the West Indies, pp. 114–119.

Young, Ruth C., 1976. "The Structural Context of Caribbean Agriculture: A Comparative Study." *Journal of Developing Areas* 10 (July):425–445.

Documents and Reports

Ali, Desmond A., 1973. *Food Processing and Food Packaging in Trinidad and Tobago.* St. Augustine, Trinidad: Caribbean Industrial Research Institute.

Asociacion Latinoamericana de Libro Comercio, 1971. "Aspectos de la Integración Agricola a Través de la ALALC." Washington, D.C.: Document presentado al Seminario de Integración Agricola, Banco Interamericano de Desarrollo.

Barbados Marketing Corporation, 1977. *The Barbados Marketing Corporation.* Bridgetown, Barbados: Leftwich Press.

Bruce, Carlton, 1978. *The Caribbean Food and Nutrition Institute: An Economic Framework.* Kingston, Jamaica: Caribbean Food and Nutrition Institute.

Bruce, Carlton J., and Rankine, Lloyd B., 1979. *A Model for the Development and Implementation of the Caribbean Food and Nutrition Plan.* Kingston, Jamaica: Caribbean Food and Nutrition Institute.

_____, 1980. *A Model for the Development and Implementation of the Regional Food and Nutrition Strategy: An Operational Framework.* Georgetown, Guyana: CARICOM Secretariat.

Buckmire, George E., 1971. "Agriculture in the CARIFTA Economic Integration Movement." Washington, D.C.: Inter-American Development Bank (Document submitted to the Seminar on Agricultural Integration).

Campbell, L. G., et al., 1976. *Agricultural Credit in General: Rural Development and the Credit Strategy for Small Farmers in the LDCs of the Caribbean.* Paramaribo, Surinam: Caribbean Development Bank, Seminar on Agricultural Credit for Small Farmers.

Capurro, Norberto L., 1971. "La Corporacíon Andina de Fomento y el Proceso de Integracíon Agricola." Washington, D.C.: Banco Interamericano de Desarrollo, Informe preparado para el Seminario de Integracíon Agricola.

Caribbean Agricultural Research and Development Institute, 1976a. *Summary of Work Programme.* St. Augustine, Trinidad.

_____, 1976b. *CARDI—Some Constraints to Development.* St. Augustine, Trinidad.

Caribbean Community Secretariat, 1977. *CARICOM Feeds Itself: Basic Answers to the Questions Most Often Asked About the Regional Food Plan.* Georgetown, Guyana: CARICOM Secretariat.

Caribbean Development Bank, 1972. *CDB Agricultural Policy in the Less Developed Countries of the Eastern Caribbean.* Bridgetown, Barbados: CDB (Technical Report No. 7).

_____, 1979. *Annual Report 1978.* Bridgetown, Barbados: CDB.

_____, 1980a. *Annual Report 1979.* Bridgetown, Barbados: CDB.

————, 1980b. *Small Farming in the Less Developed Countries of the Commonwealth Caribbean.* Bridgetown, Barbados: CDB (Report prepared by Weir's Agricultural Consulting Service, Jamaica).

————, 1981a. *Annual Report 1980.* Bridgetown, Barbados: CDB.

————, 1981b. *Agriculture. Sector Policy Paper.* Bridgetown, Barbados: CDB.

————, 1982. *Annual Report 1981.* Bridgetown, Barbados: CDB.

————, 1983. *Annual Report 1982.* Bridgetown, Barbados: CDB.

————, 1984. *Annual Report 1983.* Bridgetown, Barbados: CDB.

Caribbean Food Corporation, 1981. "Profile of the Caribbean Food Corporation." Port of Spain, Trinidad: CFC.

————, 1982. *Caribbean Food Corporation: Review of CFC's Role in Relation to Regional Food and Nutrition Strategy.* Port of Spain, Trinidad: CFC.

Caribbean Food and Nutrition Institute, 1969. *Conference on Protein Foods for the Caribbean, 1968.* Georgetown, Guyana: Proceedings of the Conference.

————, 1975a. *Available Data on the State of Food and Nutrition of the Peoples of the Commonwealth Caribbean.* Georgetown, Guyana.

————, 1975b. *Guideline to Food and Dietary Services in the Contemporary Caribbean.* Bridgetown, Barbados: CFNI (Report of a CFNI Technical Group Meeting on Food and Dietary Services).

————, Committee on Recommended Dietary Allowances, 1976. *Recommended Dietary Allowances for the Caribbean.* Mona, Jamaica: CFNI.

Caribbean Free Trade Association, Commonwealth Caribbean Regional Secretariat, 1971. *Agricultural Trade and Development in the Commonwealth Caribbean.* Georgetown, Guyana (Report of a Joint CCRS/FAO mission, prepared by P. Lamartine Yates and George E. Buckmire).

————, 1971. *CARIFTA and the New Caribbean.* Georgetown, Guyana: Commonwealth Caribbean Secretariat.

————, 1972. *From CARIFTA to Caribbean Community.* Georgetown, Guyana: Commonwealth Caribbean Secretariat.

————, 1973. *The Caribbean Community—A Guide.* Georgetown, Guyana: CARICOM Secretariat.

————, 1977. *CARICOM Feeds Itself: Basic Answers to the Questions Most Often Asked About the Regional Food Plan.* Georgetown, Guyana.

————, 1979. *A Digest of Trade Statistics of Caribbean Community Member States 1976,* rev. ed. Georgetown, Guyana: CARICOM Secretariat.

————, 1980. *CARICOM Regional Food and Nutrition Strategy: A Strategy for the 1980s.* Georgetown, Guyana: CARICOM Secretariat.

————, 1981. *The Caribbean Community in the 1980s.* Georgetown, Guyana: CARICOM Secretariat.

CARICOM Secretariat and Economic Commission for Latin America, 1977. *Study of the Payments Arrangements for AMP Trade.* Port of Spain, Trinidad: ECLA/POS.

Council for Mutual Economic Assistance, Secretariat, 1970. *Information on the Main Areas of Activity of the CMEA in the Sphere of Agriculture and Food Industry.* Moscow: CMEA.

Cropper, J.; Sammy, G. M.; and Wiltshire, W. W., 1973. *Food Processing and the Interdependence of Agriculture and Industry with Particular Reference to Fruits and Vegetables.* St. Augustine, Trinidad: Caribbean Industrial Research Institute.

Cumberbatch, E.R. St. J., 1974. *Report on Visit to Trinidad and Tobago.* Bridgetown, Barbados: Barbados Agricultural Development Corporation.

Development Management Consultants, 1980. *An Evaluation of the Farm Improvement Credit Scheme.* Bridgetown, Barbados: CDB.

Food and Agricultural Organization, 1976. *Agriculture in Regional Integration: Report of a Discussion of Comparative Experiences in Practical National Agricultures,* Seminar on Agriculture in Regional Integration. Rome: FAO.

Garvey, G.V.J., and Hoad, R. M., 1975. *Commercial Yam Production in Barbados.* Bridgetown, Barbados: Barbados Agricultural Development Corporation.

Government of Barbados, Ministry of Finance and Planning, 1980. *Barbados Development Plan 1979-83: Planning for Growth.* Bridgetown, Barbados: Government Printing Office.

Government of Belize, Central Planning Unit, 1980. *Economic Plan of Belize 1980-1983.* Belmopan, Belize: Government Printers.

Government of Belize, Ministry of Natural Resources, Department of Agriculture, 1980. *A Summary of Statistics 1979.* Belmopan, Belize: Government Printers.

Government of Guyana, 1977. *Draft Agricultural Development Plan 1978-81.* Georgetown, Guyana: Government Printers.

Government of Guyana, Ministry of Agriculture, 1980. *Crop and Livestock Statistics in Guyana: A Compilation of Existing Data.* Georgetown, Guyana: Inter-American Institute of Agricultural Sciences.

Government of Jamaica, Ministry of Agriculture, 1976. *Caribbean Food Corporation.* Kingston, Jamaica: Government Printery (Ministry Paper No. 46).

Government of Jamaica, Ministry of Agriculture, 1971. *Agricultural Sector Study—Sector Brief: Land Use and Development.* Kingston, Jamaica: Government Printery.

Government of Montserrat, 1980. *Five Year Draft Plan 1979-1983: Agricultural Sector.* Plymouth, Montserrat: Government Printery.

Government of Trinidad and Tobago and Caribbean Food and Nutrition Institute, 1970. *Interim Report on National Household Food Consumption Survey in Trinidad and Tobago.* Port of Spain, Trinidad: Government Printery.

Guyana Agricultural and General Workers' Union, 1979. *Agricultural Workers and Development.* Georgetown, Guyana.

Heaton, L., et al., 1974. *Coordinated Agricultural Development Project for Trinidad and Tobago.* Washington, D.C.: FAO/IDB Cooperative Program.

Inter-American Development Bank, 1971. "Considerations on Agricultural Trade and Development in the Economic Integration of Latin America."

Selected Bibliography 123

Washington, D.C.: IDB (Document submitted by the IDB for the Seminar on Agricultural Integration).

———, 1975. *Statistical Data on the Latin American and Caribbean Countries.* Washington, D.C.: IDB.

———, Office of the Integration Advisor, 1972. *Seminario de Integracion agricola.* Washington, D.C.: IDB.

———, Project Analysis Department, 1977a. *Participation of the Bank in the Development of Agriculture in Latin America.* Washington, D.C.: IDB.

———, Project Analysis Department, 1977b. *Participation of the Bank in the Development of Agriculture in Latin America.* Washington, D.C.: IDB.

International Bank for Reconstruction and Development, 1978. *Regional Agricultural Development and Food Production in the Caribbean.* Washington, D.C.: IBRD (Report no. 2064-CRB).

———, 1980a. *Economic Memorandum on Antigua.* Washington, D.C.: IBRD (Report no. 2928-CRG).

———, 1980b. *Economic Memorandum on Belize.* Washington, D.C.: IBRD (Report no. 2909-BEL).

———, 1980c. *Economic Memorandum on Dominica.* Washington, D.C.: IBRD (Report no. 2923-CRG).

———, 1980d. *Economic Memorandum on Grenada.* Washington, D.C.: IBRD (Report no. 2949-GRD).

———, 1980e. *Economic Memorandum on Guyana.* Washington, D.C.: IBRD (Report no. 3015-GUA).

———, 1980f. *Economic Memorandum on Montserrat.* Washington, D.C.: IBRD (Report no. 2943-MO).

———, 1980g. *Economic Memorandum on St. Kitts-Nevis.* Washington, D.C.: IBRD (Report no. 2948-CRG).

———, 1980h. *Economic Memorandum on St. Vincent and the Grenadines.* Washington, D.C.: IBRD (Report no. 2935-CRG).

———, International Development Agency, 1975. *Caribbean Regional Study.* Washington, D.C.: IBRD (Report no. 566A).

Jamaica Development Bank, 1977. *Self-Supporting Farmers' Development Programme: Socio-economic Evaluation Report.* Kingston, Jamaica: Government Printery.

Kennard, Gavin B., 1977. *Rationalisation of Research in Agriculture and Related Fields.* Georgetown, Guyana: Agricultural Communications Office.

Lewis, W. Arthur, 1936. *The Evolution of the Peasantry in the British West Indies.* London: Colonial Office (Pamphlet 656).

Meissner, Frank, 1971. "Marketing as a Tool of Integration of the Agricultural Sector of Latin America," Washington, D.C.: IDB (Document presented to the Conference on Agriculture and Regional Integration).

Pan American Health Organization, 1972. *The National Food and Nutrition Survey of Barbados, 1972.* Washington, D.C.: Pan American Union (Scientific Publication no. 237).

Phillips, Winston J., 1978. "Towards a Common Agricultural Policy for the Caribbean Community." Port of Spain, Trinidad (Paper prepared for the

Caribbean Community Secretariat/UNDP Multi-Sectoral Regional Planning Conference on a Common Agricultural Policy for the Caribbean Community).

Republic of Trinidad and Tobago, Ministry of Agriculture, Lands, and Fisheries, 1979. *White Paper on Agriculture.* Port of Spain, Trinidad: Government Printery.

Secretariat para el integracíon economica centro americana (SIECA), 1971. "El Sector Agrícola en el Proceso de Integracíon Económica Centroamericana." Washington, D.C.: IDB (Documento presentado por SIECA para el Seminario de Integración Agricola [Document presented by SIECA for the Seminar on Agricultural Integration]).

Smith, Louis L., 1974. *Critical Evaluation of the Performance of the ECCM Countries Under the Agricultural Marketing Protocol (AMP) and the Guaranteed Market Scheme (GMS).* Port of Spain, Trinidad: United Nations (ECLA, Office for the Caribbean, ECLA/POS74/16).

St. Kitts Sugar Association, Ltd., 1961. *Report on the Sugar Industry of St. Kitts, 1948–1959.* Basseterre, St. Kitts: St. Kitts Sugar Association.

United Nations/Economic Commission for Latin America, 1969. *Report of the Caribbean Regional Workshop on Integrated Rural Development.* Kingston, Jamaica: United Nations (E/CN.12/846).

———, 1969. *Report of the Caribbean Regional Workshop on Integrated Rural Development.* Kingston, Jamaica: United Nations (E/CN.12/846).

———, Office for the Caribbean, 1979. *Report on a Farm Survey Conducted in Grenada.* Port of Spain, Trinidad: United Nations (CEPAL/CARIB 79/12).

———, Office for the Caribbean, 1980. *Economic Activity 1979 in Caribbean Countries.* Port of Spain, Trinidad: United Nations (CEPAL/CARIB 80/5).

———, Office for the Caribbean, 1981. *Economic Activity 1980 in Caribbean Countries.* Port of Spain, Trinidad: United Nations (CEPAL/CARIB81/10).

———, Office for the Caribbean, 1982a. *Agricultural Statistics, Caribbean Countries 1982.* Port of Spain, Trinidad: CEPAL/CARIB 82/13.

———, Office for the Caribbean, 1982b. *Economic Activity 1981 in Caribbean Countries.* Port of Spain, Trinidad: United Nations CEPAL/CARIB82/10.

United Nations/Food and Agriculture Organization, 1971. *The Agricultural Economy of Trinidad and Tobago.* Santiago, Chile: United Nations.

———, 1976. *Agricultural Credit in the Caribbean Area.* Rome: Seminar for Selected Countries in the Caribbean Area on Credit for Small Farmers.

United States Department of Agriculture, 1974. "Indices of Agricultural Production for the Western Hemisphere, Excluding the United States and Cuba, 1965 Through 1974." *Statistical Bulletin,* no. 540.

Williams, Eric, 1974. "The Caribbean Food Crisis." Port of Spain, Trinidad: Office of the Prime Minister (Address to the Caribbean Veterinary Association, August 12, 1974).

Wirth, Carlos A., 1971. "La Agricultura y la Integracíon Económica en los Paises de la ALALC." Washington, D.C.: IDB (Document submitted to the Seminar on Agricultural Integration).

Yudelman, Montague, 1971. "New Technology for Agriculture and Economic Integration." Washington, D.C.: IDB (Document submitted to the Seminar on Agricultural Integration).

Index